A DICTIONARY OF BRITISH BIRD PAINTERS

A Dictionary of

BRITISH BIRD PAINTERS

FRANK LEWIS

F. LEWIS, PUBLISHERS, LTD
PUBLISHERS BY APPOINTMENT TO THE LATE QUEEN MARY
The Tithe House, Leigh-on-Sea, England

PRINTED AND MADE IN ENGLAND

SBN 85317 027 4

First Published 1974

PRODUCED BY F. LEWIS, PUBLISHERS LTD, AND PRINTED AT
THE DAEDALUS PRESS, STOKE FERRY, KING'S LYNN, NORFOLK

Preface

THE PRESENT century has witnessed a revolution in the appreciation of the fine arts and in our own British School in particular. Having in my capacity as a publisher issued several dictionaries devoted to specific specialised fields, i.e., Animal; Flower and Still Life; Landscape; Marine; Military; Sporting; and Victorian; it is my pleasure to add yet another to these. So this, the first Dictionary devoted entirely to British Bird Painters, comes into being – it is too much to hope that every possible name has been included. So I should, therefore, welcome information of any omissions, or additional facts, for future addition. The chronology adopted is from the earliest known British bird artist, Francis Barlow (1626-1704), to those living in this present year of grace and it will be seen that these are many, due to an enormous increase in not only bird paintings, but in the study of wild life and its conservation. I take this opportunity to acknowledge my indebtedness to the many artists who so kindly provided their biographical details and permission to make use of the data herein assembled. Also I am exceedingly grateful to those of my friends in the art world who gave both information and photographs.

Leigh-on-Sea
1974

FRANK LEWIS

Abbreviations

*	Illustrated
A.G.	Art Gallery
b.	Born
B.I.	British Institution (1806-1867)
B.M.	British Museum
coll.	Collection
d.	Died
exhib.	Exhibited
F.S.	Free Society of Artists (1761-1783)
G.G.	Grosvenor Gallery (1878-1890)
Grant	Chronological History of the Old English Landscape Painters
Inst.	Institute
lit.	Literature
Mus.	Museum
N.E.A.C.	New English Art Club
N.G.	New Gallery (1888-1893)
N.W.C.S.	New Water Colour Society (1832-1893). Now R.I.
op.	Operating
O.W.C.S.	Old Water Colour Society (1805-)
repr.	Reproduced
R.A.	Royal Academy (1769-)
R.B.A.	Royal Society of British Artists (1824-)
R.E.	Royal Society of Painter-Eetchers
R.H.A.	Royal Hibernian Academy
R.I.	Royal Institute of Painters in Water-colours
R.M.S.	Royal Society of Miniature Painters
R.S.A.	Royal Scottish Academy (1826-)
R.S.M.A.	Royal Society of Marine Artists
R.S.P.B.	Royal Society for the Protection of Birds
S.A.	Society of Artists (1760-1791)
S & D	Signed and dated
S.S.	Suffolk Street Galleries
S.W.A.	Society of Women Artists
S.W.L.A.	Society of Wild Life Artists
V & A	Victoria & Albert Museum
V.E.	Various exhibitions

** Denotes illustrated example of the artist shown.*

ADAMS, DOUGLAS. op. 1880-1905
London address (7 James Street, Haymarket). Landscape and wildfowl painter, occasionally sport.
Exhib. R.A. (18); S.S. (6); G.G. (2); N.G. (5); V.E. (3).

AGASSE, JACQUES LAURENT. b. Geneva 1767, d. London 1849
Son of a Huguenot aristocrat. Presumed to have studied animals in his father's stables. Came to London in 1800 with a reputation as an animal painter so should not be considered as a bird painter, but he painted everything and a sheet of studies of Owls, Peahen etc. in the Paul Mellon collection qualifies him for an entry herein. But he was more than this, an artist of great and varied power, painting both open-air genre and scenes of sport and the road, all in finely-executed landscape, and in a broad technique entirely his own.
Exhib. R.A. (29); B.I. (7); R.B.A. (5).

AINSLIE, Miss. op. 1823-1835
Hon. exhibitor at Royal Academy. No address given. Painted game birds and sporting subjects.
Exhib. R.A. (11).

ALEXANDER, EDWIN., R.S.A., R.W.S. b. Edinburgh 1870, d. Musselburgh 1926
Eldest son of Robert Alexander, R.S.A. Scottish painter of flowers, birds and animals. Studied art at Edinburgh and in Paris under Fremiet. Visited Tangier with his father and Joseph Crawhall (q.v.). Visited Egypt in 1895 and 1902. Many of his water colours are painted on silk, linen and textured paper. His style reflects the Glasgow School and the influence of Japanese Art.
Exhib. R.S.A. Centenary exhibition 1926 (5).
Coll. Edinburgh, Glasgow, Preston, Tate Gallery.
Lit. *Art Journal* 1905.

ALEXANDER, Mrs. RONA ALTAN. b. Auckland, N.Z. 20th August 1905
A 'lone wolf' painting portraits of people, birds and animals wherever she happens to be. Belongs to no Art Societies. Self-taught artist painting in oils, water colours and pastel. Has executed a number of large oils of birds of New Zealand (all commissioned). Resides near Dorchester.
Exhib. Paris Salon, several London Art Societies. Has had 'one-man' exhibitions in London and New Zealand from time to time.
Coll. National Gallery of New Zealand, Wellington.
Repr. Card designs published in Britain, America, Australasia.

ANDREW, F. W., the Elder. op. 1826-1827
London address. Painted game birds.
Exhib. S.S. (3).

ANDREWS, LILIAN. b. 2nd August 1878
London address. Painter in water colour of birds and animals etc. Studied Brighton School of Art.
Exhib. R.A., R.S.A., Paris Salon (1953-55) and provincial galleries (Leeds, Bradford, Newcastle, Bournemouth, Brighton etc.).
Coll. Nottingham A.G. (mallards), Leeds A.G. (peahen and chicks).

ANGELL, Mrs. JOHN. b. 1847, op. 1875-1882.
Painter in water colours, mostly of flowers, fruit and birds, in the manner of Hunt, Clare and Cruickshank. Her works were on the small side.
Exhib. R.A., O.W.C.S., N.W.C.S., G.G.

ARMFIELD, GEORGE. op. 1840-1875
London painter of landscape, game birds and wild animals. Graves states his real name was Smith. There is also an Edward Armfield who painted like subjects and may possibly be related. His speciality was dogs chasing birds.
Exhib. R.A. (1840-1862), B.I., and S.S.

ARMITAGE, H.
A large painting (43 x 55 in.) of a 'Blackcock and grey hens on a Moor' was auctioned at Christie's 12.10.72.

ARMOUR-CHELU, IAN.
Exhib. Sladmore Gallery, London 1973 (15 bird paintings).

ATKINSON, E. b. Datchet, op. 1793-1797
London, Long Acre address.
Exhib. R.A. (3), Snipe in 1793, Woodcock in 1794.

ATKINSON, Miss MARY. op. 1833-1839
Exhib. R.A. (1); S.S. (1), (Birds).

*AUSTEN, WINIFRED, R.I., R.E. (Mrs. Frick). b. Ramsgate, d 1964
Daughter of Staff Surgeon Josiah Austin, R.N. Married Oliver O'Donnell Frick. Privately educated, studying art under Mrs. Jopling Rowe and C. E. Swan. Painter in oils and water colours of birds and animal life. Resided at Orford in Suffolk. Illustrated *Birds Ashore and Aforeshore* (Chalmers), *Marsh and Mudflat* (Dawson) and other books.
Exhib. R.A. (from 1899), R.I., R.E., Societé des Artistes Francais, etc.
Coll. Harris Museum & A.G., Preston; Ipswich A.G.

BACON, D'ARCY. op. 1855-1874
Painter of animals and his exhibited painting 'The Haunt of the Heron' gives him a notice herein.
Exhib. R.A. (1); B.I. (3); S.S. (10).

BAKER, LESLIE
Exhib. S.W.L.A. 'House Sparrows', 'Great Grey Shrike', 'Red Backed Shrike'.

BAKER, Miss. fl. 1810-1820
Cheltenham address.
Exhib. R.A. (4), (game birds).

BAKER, RICHARD. b. 1822, fl. until 1851
Painted game and landscape.
Exhib. R.H.A. 1843-1851.

BALE, C.T. op. 1868-1875
London address. Painted still life and birds, also flowers.
Exhib. R.A. (1); S.S. (15).

BALL, SYLVIA CAROLINE. b. Mark Cross, Sussex 21st June 1914.
Member S.W.L.A., exhibiting annually; also at Birdland Gallery, Burton-on-the-Water, painting in all mediums. Trained at Slade and then with the Austrian animal painter Alfons Purtscher. Signs work 'Oeuf'.

BARBER, ALFRED R. op. 1879-1893
Colchester address.
Exhib. S.S. (7); V.E. (11), (game birds).

BARBER, Mrs. ELIZABETH (née Bowker). op. 1818-1899
Painted flowers, birds, butterflies, plants, etc.
Exhib. Grahamstown, 1870.
Lit. *The Berbers of the Peak,* 1934. *Pictorial Art in South Africa* (A. Gordon Brown, 1952).

BARBUT, JAMES op. 1777-1786
Ostensibly a painter of birds and shells. These are most delicately painted, as is the landscape or seascape in which they are placed. Of these he exhibited 17 at the R.A. from addresses in the City and the Strand. A skilful artist, and an addition to the painters of his peculiar line.

BARENGER, JAMES, Junr. b. 25th December 1780, d. London 1894
Son of a painter and glazier of Kentish Town, who painted insects and bred pointers, who was also related to Woollett and Pouncy, the engravers. James Junr. is best known as a painter of sporting subjects and animals, but he did include birds (pheasants) so warrants a note in this work.

*BARLOW, FRANCIS. b. Lincolnshire 1626, d. 11th August 1704 (d. 1702 Benezit)
By instinct Barlow was a kind of English Hondecoeter. For him the skies and meads existed for the display of huge and numerous birds, usually agitated by some concern of venery, combat, love or attack from man or beast. And very masterly, one and all, are these presentiments, displaying powers in draughtsmanship and imagination, in grouping, little inferior to those of the Flemish Master (Hondecoeter, 1636-1695) who was his junior contemporary. Barlow lived long, from the reign of Charles I to the accession of Queen Anne. Barlow first studied portraiture under William Sheppard, but his taste lay to birds, fish and animals. The great 'Decoy' and 'The Farmyard' in Lord Onslow's possession, are both works crowded with birds. Though he both made money and inherited it, Drury Lane remained his address and penury his portion to the end. He was buried in St. Margaret's Churchyard, Westminster.
Coll. B.M., V. & A., Plymouth A.G., Preston A.G., Bedford A.G. and many private collections.
Repr. *Aesops Fables* (1665-1666). 110 plates etched from his own designs.
Lit. Grant, *The Old English Landscape Painters,* vol. 1, p. 56.

BARRET, Miss M. d. 1836
Daughter of George Barret, Senr. Pupil of George Romney and Mrs. Mee. Member O.W.C.S. Painted still life, birds and miniatures.
Exhib. R.A. (8); O.W.C.S. (36).

BATT, J. ARTHUR. op. 1875
Painted in an uninspiring manner, small pictures, sometimes on panels, of domestic animals and birds. Living at Romsey.
Exhib. R.A. (4); S.S. (14).

BEAUMONT, Miss A. op. 1873-
London address.
Exhib. S.S. (1), Game.

BEAVIS, MAUD. op. 1840-
London address.
Exhib. S.S. (1), Geese.

*BELL, J.C. op. 1850-1892
Newcastle and Scarborough addresses. *Not* John Clement Bell (b. 1860) of London.
Exhib. Harris Museum & A. G., Preston 1943. A 'Sheldrake' signed as above and dated 1857 and lent by the late Dr. H. J. Taylor of Preston.
Repr. *British Sporting Painters.*

*BENINGFIELD, GORDON GEORGE. b. London, October 1936
Living in Hertfordshire. Studied at St. Alban's School of Art 1953/57. Then undertook ecclesiastical sculpture and glass engraving whilst still maintaining his enthusiasm for natural history drawing. In 1967 went to Iceland where he studied bird life and gathered material for his pictures. Works in water colours highlighted with gouache and specialises in depicting the smaller mammals and birds of the English countryside. Also produces bronze sculptures.
Exhib. Moorland Gallery, London. Tryon Gallery, London. International Fine Arts Exhibition, Budapest (Diploma), 'Snipe'.
Coll. In many private collections, Great Britain, Europe, U.S.A. and Canada.

BENSTEAD, J. (Shaw Sparrow); BENSTED (Grant, Graves & Benezit). op. 1828-1847
Maidstone address. Mainly a sporting painter of animals, game birds etc. his subjects set in landscape.
Exhib. R.A. (7) including 'Dead Game', 'Snipes & Heron', 'Shot Mallard'.

BERTHOUD, HENRY. b. London 1790, d. Paris 1864.
Painter of game.
Exhib. S.S. (2).

BERTRAM, Miss. op. 1867
London address.
Exhib. S.S. 1867, (Game).

BEST, J. op. 1772-1787
A once well-known painter of game-cocks, sporting animals and prize cattle.
Exhib. R.A. (2); S.A. (7).

BEWICK, THOMAS. b. Cherryburn, Ovingham, Northumberland 1753, d. Gateshead 1828
Best known as prolific wood engraver and naturalist. Also produced a number of watercolours of birds and animals. Had a workshop in St. Nicholas' Churchyard in Newcastle-upon-Tyne which undertook a great variety of engraving including sword blades, coffin plates, tradesmen's cards, banknotes and clock faces. Bewick illustrated many books including his *Quadrupeds* and *Birds* which are now chiefly remembered for their tailpieces.
Coll. B.M.; V. & A. Studies of Birds and Fishes; Witt Library.
Repr. D. Croal Thomson; Williams.
Lit. D. Croal Thomson, 1950. *Water Colour Drawings of Thomas Bewick.*

BIDDEN, R.O. fl. 1833
London address.
Exhib. N.W.C.S. (2), game.

BIDDULPH, S.
'A Hawk attacking a Duck', signed, was sold at Sotheby's 2nd March 1960.

BINKS, Reuben Ward. b. Bolton
Living New York 1934. Known mainly as a painter of sporting scenes, in particular of sporting dogs. But he did include birds. Signs work 'Ward Binks'.
Repr. 'Canada Geese'; 'Fine Feathers' (Swans); 'River Swans' Aquatints by Frost & Reed Ltd, Bristol & London.
Exhib. 'Widgeon' w.c. British Sporting Paintings Exhibition at Preston Art Gallery, October 1943, no. 22.

BINNS, DAVID. b. Sutton-in-Craven, Yorkshire 1935
Member of S.W.L.A. working mainly in water colour, but his larger works painted in oils. Trained Skipton and Keighley Schools of Art and Leeds College of Art (Diploma). Represented in many private collections, including America and Canada.
Exhib. R.I.; S.W.L.A.; Yorkshire Artists, Leeds & Bradford; Tryon Gallery, London; Arun Art Centre; Wildfowl Trust and several other private Galleries.

BLACKWELL, Miss ELIZABETH. op. 1819
Exhib. R.A. 1819 (Birds).

BLAKE, BENJAMIN. op. 1807-1832
A noted, almost famous, painter of still life, whose dead hares, birds etc. delight the lovers of such works rather for their minuteness than their quality. His little landscapes, more frequent than is recognized, display a sweet if timid sense of scenery in the soft greens and browns in which they are carried out.
Exhib. R.A. (13); B.I. (17); R.B.A. (19).

BODKIN, FREDERICK E. op. 1872-1893
London address.
Exhib. R.A. (19); S.S. (14); N.W.C.S. (2); V.E. (36).

*BOGDANI, JACOB. b. Eperjes, Hungary, d. Finchley, London 1724
Son of a court official at Vienna, where he learnt to paint. Came to England and was appointed Court Painter to William III. Flower and Bird painter. Did work at the King's Castle at Dieren in Holland and in England for forty or fifty years.
Known as Bogdany, Bogdane or Bochdani.
Coll. Hampton Court Palace, Budapest, Stockholm, Broughton Collection, etc.
Exhib. Trafalgar Galleries, London (Nov.–Dec. 1967) 'Parrot & Wild Ducks in a Landscape'.

BOREHAM, J. *c.*1702-1714
An obscure painter whose works appear to be lost. A large canvas 60 x 33½ inches was exhibited by Leggatt Brothers in 1951. Titled 'A Choir of Birds', it depicted 19 brilliantly plumaged birds in variety perched on a tree, singing an anthem from a musical score reading *'God preserve her Majesty and forever send her V. . .'* in a landscaped background. An accomplished painting, presumably influenced by Bogdani and on stylistic grounds would appear to have been painted in the reign of Queen Anne and in this country.
Exhib. Leggatt Brothers, London, 1951.
Repr. *The Connoisseur,* March 1951, in colour.

BOUGHTON, T. op.1845-1847
Guildford address.
Exhib. S.S. (4), Game Birds.

BOUVIER, Miss J. op. 1853-1873
London address.
Exhib. S.S. (20); V.E. (3), Game.

BRADLEY, EDWARD. op.1824-1867
Painted both game birds and landscape.
Exhib. R.A. (12); B.I. (53); R.B.A. (77).

BRETT, J. op. 1858
London address.
Exhib. S.S. (2), Birds.

BRIGHT, HARRY. op. 1882
The Sladmore Gallery exhibited a S&D 1882 'Mexican Crested Eagle' by this artist. Possibly the same as Henry Bright, active *c* 1870-1877.

BRIGHT, HENRY. b. Saxmundham 1814, d. Ipswich 1873
Son of a jeweller and lapidary. Apprenticed to a Chemist at Woodbridge, Suffolk, later dispenser at Norwich Hospital. Here he became acquainted with John Berney Crome, Cotman, and other members of the Norwich School. Abandoned his appointment to become a professional artist. Went to London in 1836. Not strictly a bird painter but included birds in his repertoire.
Exhib. N.W.C.S., R.A., B.I., R.B.A. from 1836. Member N.W.C.S. in 1893, resigning in 1845.
Coll. Birmingham Art Gallery have 'A study of Snipe' and a 'Study of Woodcock'.

BRIGHT, HENRY. active *c* 1870-1877
Not to be confused with Henry Bright (1814-1873) of the Norwich School. But a painter of birds – two water colours of parrots were exhibited at the Alpine Club Gallery 14-15th March 1972.

BRITTAN, CHARLES E., Senr. op. 1860-90.

BROWN, Miss ELLA G. op. 1887-1888
Lytham address.
Exhib. R.A. (2), Game.

BROWN, R.G. op. 1844
Exhib. R.A. (1).

BROWNE, J.B. op. 1861-1863
London address.
Exhib. R.A. (1); S.S. (1).

BROWNE, RICHARD.
A water colour titled 'The Mountain Pheasant' 13 x 10 was sold at Christie's 4th October 1972.

BRUNTON, E. op. 1857
London address.
Exhib. S.S. (1), Game.

BRYMNER, WILLIAM. op. 1884
London address.
Exhib. V. E. (1), Birds.

BULLEY, ASHBURNHAM H. op. 1841-1851
Painted dogs, wildfowl etc., sometimes on large canvases.
Exhib. R.A. (3); B.I. (13); R.B.A. (7).

BULLOCK, G.G. op. 1827-1859
Many of this once favourite genre-painter's works are landscapes in all but title. He painted also portraits and dead game.
Exhib. R.A. (54); B.I. (37); R.B.A. (24).

BURBANK, J.M. op. 1825, d. 1873
This Camberwell man painted animals and birds in both oils and water colours. Known to have travelled in America.
Exhib. R.A. (12); B.I. (6); S.S. (19); N.W.C.S. (21).

BUSBY, JOHN PHILIP. b. Bradford, Yorkshire 2nd February 1928
Member Society of Wild Life Artists; Society of Scottish Artists (President 1973); The Glasgow Group of Artists; Fellow Royal Society of Arts. Exhibiting regularly with Art Societies, Arts Council (Scottish Spectrum 71). Many one-man shows in Scotland and North of England. Bird paintings and drawings represented in group shows at Reading A.G., The Oxford Gallery, and Century Galleries, Henley. Works mostly in oil on canvas, not confined to birds – often highly abstracted, concerned with a response to landscape, weather, and its symbolism. Deeply interested in animal behaviour spending much time in the field. Birds are drawn from direct experience and not as idealised bird-book objects. Delights in grouping of different species – such as occurs in sea bird colonies or in the coastal estuaries. Trained at Leeds and Edinburgh Colleges of Art. Presently teaching at Edinburgh College of Art.
Coll. Abbott Hall, Kendal; Belfast A.G.; Bradford A.G.; Glasgow A.G.; Wakefield A.G.; Scottish Arts Council; Yorks. Arts Assn.; Edinburgh Corporation; W. Riding Education Dept.; Prudential Insurance Co.; R.S.P.B.
Repr. Illustrated *Galapagos, Island of Birds* 1968 (Longman's), *Azraq, Desert Oasis* 1973 (Allen Lane), *Gannets & Boobies* (Oliver & Boyd) all by Dr. J. B. Nelson. Cover design for *Birds* (R.S.P.B. Journal) and card for British Museum of Natural History and British Trust for Ornithology.

CALDECOTT, RANDOLPH, R.I. 1846-1886
Son of a Chester accountant, his natural gift for drawing beasts and birds continued to develop while he was employed as a bank clerk in Manchester. In 1872 went to London and received commissions for drawings in several periodicals while working in the studio of Dalon, the sculptor, and at the Slade. Made quite a name for himself as an illustrator of popular children's books. Illustrated Washington Irving's *Sketch Book.*
Coll. The Tate, V.&A., Bristol A.G., Manchester A.G., Newport A.G.

CALVIN, — op. 1773
Penrith address.
Exhib. R.A. (1) Birds.

CAMPBELL, MERIEL (living)
Exhib. S.W.L.A. 'Cape Teal', 'Australian Shelduck', 'Coreopsis Goose', 'Andean Flamingo'.

CAMPION, S. op. 1831-1833
Painter of animals, birds and still life.
Exhib. R.A. (2); B.I. (6).

CASTEELS, PETER. b. Antwerp 3rd October 1684, d. Richmond 16th May 1749
Strictly a Flemish painter but he visited England in 1708 remaining here for the next 41 years, so most of his painting life was in England and therefore qualifies for an entry here. Painted flowers, fruit and birds and also engraved. Published twelve plates of birds and fowl in 1726.

CATESBY, MARK. b. 1679, d. 1749
Pupil of Joseph Goupy. Visited North America 1710-1719 and again in 1722-1726. Published *The Natural History of Carolina* (London, 1731-1743 in 2 volumes).
Lit. *Mark Catesby's Natural History of Carolina, Florida and the Bahamas.* Portfolio of 50 colour plates 1971 (The Beehive Press, Savanah, Georgia). 220 monochrome plates plus 50 in colour.
Coll. H.M. The Queen.
Exhib. London, National Book League (1950).

CATFORD, NANCY (Mrs. J.R. Stone). b. London 31st August 1905 (living)
Mainly woodcarver but does exhibit drawings and pastels from time to time, painting in water colour, pastel and black and white. Sculptor member of the Society of Wild Life Artists (1964), also Red Rose Guild, Manchester (since 1934). Trained at St. Alban's School of Art, and School of Woodcarving, South Kensington.
Coll. Stoke-on-Trent A.G.
Illus. R. M. Lockley's *Puffins.* Children's books for Fredk. Muller, Odhams Press, Hulton's and Daily Mail.

CHANTRY, N. op. 1797-1838
A painter of still life, game and some genre, but also of several coastal landscapes which appeared at the R.A. and B.I.

CHATFIELD, Rev. H. op. 1781-1801
Exhibited at the R.A. two paintings of game birds.

CHILD, W. or R. op. 1783-1788
Eltham address.
Exhib. R.A. (4).

CHRISTMAN, JOHN CHRISTOPHER. op. 1776-1783
An obscure but skilful painter of birds seen in landscapes of execution as pretty as is theirs. A Kingfisher of his, done in 1780, glows with fine but restrained colour.
Exhib. R.A. (1); S.A. (3); F.S. (1).

CLARKE, FREDERICK. op. 1834-1870
Resident in London and Leicester.
Exhib. R.A. (10), Game.

COLEMAN, EDWARD. b. Birmingham *c*1795, d. *c*1867
Birmingham address. Painted game and kindred subjects.
Coll. Birmingham A.G. (3).
Exhib. R.A. (16), Game Birds.

*COLLINS, CHARLES. 1680-1744
An important early painter of birds and animals of the time of Barlow and Cradock, little is known of his life. His style had the precision of a miniaturist. He was adept at catching the characteristic pose of a bird. In 1736 Fletcher & Mynde engraved a set of 12 plates of 100 British birds made from his drawings.
Coll. National Gallery of Ireland; The Royal Collection; Bedford A.G.
Exhib. Spink's, London (Nov./Dec. 1968) Red Parakeets S&D 1742/3.

COLLYER, W. op. 1820
London address.
Exhib. R.A. (1), game.

COMPLIN, George. op. 1791-1795
At the Derby Porcelain Factory 1791-1795. A fruit and flower painter who interposed birds and squirrels in his decorations; the following are some of his factory patterns:
No. 237. Fruit and Birds
No. 245. Fruit with Tom-tit and Bullfinch before dark landscape
No. 254, 259, 261, 325. Fruit and Birds
No. 349. Landskip (sic) with pair of Goldfinches and nest and two Bullfinches
(the above from the 'Cup and Saucer Book')
No. 159. Birds and Landskip (sic). From the 'Plate Book'
Lit. *Crown Derby Porcelain* by F. B. Gilhespy. Lewis Publishers 1951.

COOK, J. op. 1808-1809
London address.
Exhib. R.A. (2).

COOK, JOSHUA. op. 1838-1848
Painter of birds, game, fruit, cattle and sporting scenes. Some were on large canvases.
Exhib. R.A. (8); B.I. (14); R.B.A. (5).

COOKE, ERNEST O. op. 1886
London address.
Exhib. R.A. (1), Birds.

*COOMBS, Dr. CHARLES JOHN FRANKLIN, M.A., M.B., B.Ch. b. Bristol 27th December 1908
Educated Clifton College and Trinity Hall, Cambridge (Medicine & Natural Sciences). Medical practice in Cornwall for over 30 years. President Cornwall Bird Watching & Preservation Society. President Cornwall Naturalists Trust Ltd. Member of Council of British Ornithologists Union 1962-65. Ornithological interests include research in Avian Physiology and behaviour, Conservation, Painting & Book illustration. Founder member S.W.L.A. Paints in oils, water colour and gouache.
Coll. Ulster Museum; Lancaster University Biology Dept.
Exhib. S.W.L.A., Tryon Gallery, Nairobi, etc.

COOPER, EDWIN (of Beccles). b. Beccles, op. 1803-1831
A painter of horses, sporting scenes and coaching subjects. But he did paint cocks and cock fighting. 'A Cock Fight' was in the now dispersed Hutchinson collection, and Frost & Reed Ltd, London, in a collection of 18th & 19th Century Sporting Paintings, exhibited a pair of cock-fighting pictures 'Set to' and 'The Death' both S & D 1816. Edward Cooper with same dates is probably the same, probably responsible for the assumption of E for Edward, as several painting are signed E. Cooper.

COOPER, WILLIAM. (living)
Illustrated *Parrots of the World* by Joseph Forshaw (1973) with paintings of 500 different birds in their natural settings.

CORBOULD, ALFRED. op. 1831-1875
One of a numerous family of artists. A painter of animals and game of considerable note and skill both with beasts and their landscape surroundings. He studied horses at Tattersall's famous sale ring, then in Grosvenor Place.
Exhib. R.A. (21); B.I. (21); R.B.A. (16).

CORRIE, Miss E.J. op. 1877
Exeter address.
Exhib. R.A. (1), Game.

COXWELL, A.F. op. 1869
Bracknell address.
Exhib. V.E. (1), Ducks.

*CRADOCK, MARMADUKE. b. Somerton near Ilchester 1660, d. London 1717
Not Luke, as long described. This old painter of birds, especially ducks and other waterfowl, was a close follower of Francis Barlow (q.v.), at least in subjects. He may be distinguished from his exemplar by a bolder and more strongly coloured technique, which, if coarser in handling, renders his canvases very decorative objects of their kind. The landscape in which he sets his lively fowl, these often pursued by a hawk or quarrelling amongst themselves, is sweetly painted, with a truthful sense of aspect of fens and farmlands of Carolean England. Like Barlow's, his work is rare.
Coll. London, Painters' Hall; British Museum.
Lit. Grant, *Old English Landscape Painters* vol. 1, 1957 ed.
Exhib. 'Birds on a Pool' Leger Gallery (Nov./Dec. 1970, illus. cat.).

CRAIG, H. op. 1815
London address.
Exhib. R.A. (1), Birds.

CRAWHALL, JOSEPH. b. Morpeth, Northumberland 20th August 1861, d. London 24th May 1913
Painter in water-colour of birds and animals. Trained by his father, then studied art at King's College, London, and later under Aime Morot in Paris. Awarded Gold Medal at Munich, Silver Medal at Paris. He was influenced by oriental art.
Exhib. R.A. (from 1883); Laing A.G., Newcastle, 1951; First one-man exhibition at Alex. Reid's Gallery, Glasgow, 1894; International Society 1898-1913.
Coll. Burrell Collection, Glasgow; Tate Gallery 'The Dove'.
Lit. *Joseph Crawhall: The Man & the Artist* by Adrian Bury, 1958.

CRESWELL, J. op. 1857
London address.
Exhib. R.A. (1), Birds.

CRUIKSHANK, WILLIAM (Graves says Cruickshank). b. 1844/48, d. 1922
Painter of still-life, game and birds. Imitated W. H. Hunt.
Exhib. R.A. (7); S.S. (22).
Coll. Harris Museum & Art Gallery, Preston.

CURRIE, ROBERT. op.1880-1885.
Methven, N.B. address.
Exhib. R.A. (1); V.E. (2), Birds.

CUSA, NOEL WILLIAM. b. Hull 25th December 1909
Member M.A.F.A. and S.W.L.A. Painting in both water colour and oils.
Exhib. M.A.F.A., R.I., R.O.I., S.W.L.A.
Coll. Belfast A.G., Reading Museum & A.G.

DALTON, Mrs. M. op. 1879
London address.
Exhib. R.A. (2), Birds.

DANIEL, C.G. op. 1837
Exhib. R.A. (1), Game Birds.

DANNER, J. op. 1830
London address.
Exhib. S.S. (2), Game Birds.

DAVIES, W. op. 1819
Exhib. R.A. (4), Game.

DAVIS, WILLIAM. op. 1851-1878
Painted game, landscape and fruit.
Exhib. R.A. (16); S.S. (1); V.E. (3).

DAYSON, L. J. op. 1855
Exhib. S.S. (1), Ducks.

DEHAUSSY, Madame. op. 1851
Exhib. B.I. (2), Birds.

DELOTZ, G.G. op. 1848-1864
London address.
Exhib. R.A. (4); S.S. (2). All Game Birds.

DENNIS, WILLIAM. op.1834-1849
Exhib. R.A. (4); S.S. (7); V.E. (8), Game Birds.

DENT, Miss J. op.1869
Exhib. S.S. (1), Birds.

DETMOLD, CHARLES MAURICE, A.R.E. b. 21st November 1883, d. 9th April 1908
Twin brother to Edward Julius D. They both specialised in etchings and drawings of fish, birds and other animals, many of which were produced in collaboration. They illustrated Rudyard Kipling's *Jungle Book,* issued in 1903. In 1900 an exhibition of their work was held at the premises of The Fine Art Society, London.
Coll. V. & A. (drawings).

*DETMOLD, EDWARD JULIUS, A.R.E. b. 21st November 1883, d. 1957
Twin brother to Charles Maurice D. and both painted similar subjects (see Charles Maurice D.). Both exhibited at the Royal Academy at the age of 13. Also both were elected in 1904 Associates of the Royal Society of Painter Etchers and Engravers.
Exhib. The Fine Art Society (May 1900) (both brothers).

DEXTER, W. op. 1840-1855
Graves gives him with a Boston, U.S.A. address, so he should not be confused with the Derby Porcelain Decorator.
Exhib. R.A. (3); B.I. (1); S.S. (3), all Birds.

DEXTER, WILLIAM. op. 1830-1855
Painted flowers, fruit, butterflies and birds at the Derby Porcelain Manufactory. Travelled frequently between London and France.
Lit. Gilhespy *Crown Derby Porcelain.*

DICKES, WILLIAM. op. 1843-1881
London address. Illustrated a number of works dealing with birds.

DICKINSON, Miss H. op. 1803
Exhib. R.A. (1); V.E. (1), Birds.

DIGBY, R.D.
Exhib. Sladmore Gallery, London (December 1973), 'Bearded Tits', 'Sparrow Hawks'.

*DIXON, SAMUEL. op. 1748, d. 1769
Resident of Dublin and son of Thomas Dixon, a hosier. Dixon is said to have been the greatest exponent of the art of embossed bird painting. In 1757 he sold all his stock in Dublin and went to London, opening a picture shop. He finally returned to Dublin in 1768. A series of 22 embossed bird and flower paintings by this 18th century painter fetched the sum of £22,675 at Christie's in 1973. These formerly belonged to Cicely, Marchioness of Zetland. Two of them fetched 1,600 guineas each.
Exhib. Dublin Society of Artists.
Coll. Howth Castle; Mr. J. C. Quilter.
Lit. 'Embossed pictures of Samuel Dixon' by A. K. Longfield (*Country Life* 5th December 1966). Strickland, *Dictionary of Irish Artists.*

DODSON, RICHARD. op. 1815-1825
He was apprenticed at the Royal Crown Derby Porcelain Factory and worked there from about 1815-1825. He painted birds only which were drawn with a landscape background.

DOE, WILLIAM. (19th century)
Painted birds, feathers and insects at the Worcester Porcelain Manufactory.

DOUGHTY, DOROTHY. b. San Remo 1892, d. October 1962
Famous for her series of birds modelled for Worcester Royal Porcelain Factory. Studied at Eastbourne School of Art. Journey through the United States of America producing drawings for her bird subjects.

DOW, LUMLEY. op. 1893
Exhib. V.E. (1), Game.

DUFFIELD, WILLIAM. b. Bath 1816, d. London 1863
Pupil of George Lance. Painter of flowers, fruit and still-life. Produced a number of bird paintings.

*EDE, BASIL. b. Fetcham, Surrey 12th February 1931
Probably the finest living painter of wild birds, an acknowledged master in the art of portraying them. As a Ship's Purser regularly visiting the Far East he was drawn to Oriental Art and one might say it was his inspiration. In 1958 he emerged in the art world with his first London exhibition at the Rowland Ward Gallery, followed by five exhibitions at the The Tryon Gallery, London in 1960, 1962, 1964, 1965 & 1968. These were followed by a collection of his work being shown at the Smithsonian Institution, Washington D.C. sponsored by the British Embassy, the Audubon Society and the English Speaking Union. Then in 1966 and 1971 Kennedy Galleries Inc, New York arranged exhibitions of his work. Also in 1966 his works were exhibited at the Pieter Wenning Gallery, Johannesburg, this was part of a large World Wild Life Fund exhibition. He is a member of the Society of Wild Life Artists.
Coll. H.R.H. Prince Philip, Duke of Edinburgh. The Hon. Walter Annenberg, American Ambassador to Court of St. James. National Collection of Fine Arts, Smithsonian Institution, Washington D.C. Gulf States Paper Corporation, Tuscaloosa, U.S.A. The Ulster Museum, N. Ireland, etc.
Repr. 'Birds of Town and Country' (*Country Life,* London 1965). *Sounds of Mystery* (Holt Rinehart & Winston Inc, New York). Prints of his paintings published by Royle Publications Ltd., The Medici Society Ltd., The Donald Art Co. Inc., Janus House Inc., and Graphic Arts Inc, (the last three in U.S.A.).

EDWARDS, GEORGE. b. Stratford 1694, d. Plaistow 1773
Travelled on the Continent 1716-1731. Librarian to the College of Physicians 1733. Wrote on Natural History. Painter of birds and animals.
Repr. *A Natural History of Uncommon Birds and Animals* 1747-1751. *Gleanings of Natural History* 1758-1764.

*EDWARDS, JOHN, F.S.A. op. 1763-1812
Brentford address. Member Society of Artists. A painting of Game exhibited at the R.A. in 1797 was probably by this artist.
Exhib. S.A. (53); F.S. (4); B.I. (1).
Repr. Preston Museum & A.G. *Pictures from Lytham Hall* 1955-56. *British Herbal* 1770. *Collection of Flowers Drawn after Nature* 1783-1795.

EDWARDS, SYDENHAM. b. *c*1768, d. 8th February 1819
Draughtsman of plants and animals.
Repr. *Cynographia Britannica* 1800-1805. *New Flora Britannica,* 1818. Made drawings for other works.
Coll. V. & A., 'Solitary Snipe of Nepal' and 'Woodcock'.

ELDRIDGE, MILDRED. (living)
The Medici Society have reproduced studies of birds by this artist, as a card.

ELLIS, MALCOLM. b. London July 1940
Self-taught bird painter, studying the work of the established artists. Keeper at London Zoo for several years, resigning to become a full-time freelance bird painter specialising principally in illustrating. Spent some time studying birds in Africa, and the bird life of Africa has become his special interest.
Exhib. S.W.L.A.
Illus. *Eagles, Hawks and Falcons of the World* (Country Life); *African Birds of Prey* (Collins); *Eagles* (Arthur Barker); *The World of Birds* (Hamlyn); *A Field Guide to the Birds of East Africa* (Sapra Studio, Nairobi); co-author of *Animals of the World – Africa* (Hamlyn) and *The Treasury of Birds* (Octopus Books). Regular contributor to the weekly journal *Cage and Aviary Birds.*

ELMER, STEPHEN, A.R.A. b. 1717, d. Farnham 1796
A Farnham maltster's son, he continued in the business while gaining a high reputation as a painter of animals, birds, rural scenes and still life. His bird pictures, especially of game birds, were true to life, accurately drawn and of artistic merit. Like Charles Collins he could catch the characteristic pose of a bird. He had a bold and free style which gives his paintings individuality. Member of Society of Artists in 1763, in 1772 sent 9 pictures of animals, birds and fish to the R.A. and was made an A.R.A. He was then considered the most successful British painter of still life and dead game.
Exhib. R.A. (117); Free Society (113).
Auct. 'Two Cock Pheasants' at Sotheby's, 23rd March 1972.

ELMER, WILLIAM. op. 1780-1799
Presumed nephew of Stephen Elmer, with whom he lived at Farnham. Painted the same subject in the same style and Colonel M. H. Grant concedes that, if unsigned, their work is hard to distinguish. Visited Ireland working there for a while.
Exhib. R.A. (6), between 1783-1799; S.S. (19).

*ELSWORTH, ALFRED. op. 1889
A fine landscape scene with geese and turkeys S&D 1889 canvas 30 x 50 ins., was shown at the Oscar & Peter Johnson Ltd Galleries in November 1973. The whole, especially the birds, very expertly painted.

*ENNION, ERIC ARNOLD ROBERTS, M.A., M.R.C.S., L.R.C.P. b. Kettering 1900
Probably the most widely known of living British bird painters. Gave up medical practice (Cambs.) in 1944 to become Warden of first Field Centre of Field Study Council at Flatford Mill. From 1951-61 Director of own Field Station and Bird Observatory (Monks House, Northumberland). Now in active retirement in Wiltshire. Founder member and Chairman of Society of Wild Life Artists. Best described as author/co-author /illustrator of some twenty books, mostly natural history. Lecturer and Tutor.
Exhib. R.B.A., Suffolk Street and Mall Galleries; Greatorex Gallery; Ackermann's Gallery, London, and many provincial Galleries in both one-man and joint exhibitions.

ENSOR, MARY (Mrs. HENRY). op. 1871-1874
Resident in Birkenhead. Obscure painter of flowers and birds, known only by her seven exhibits at the S.S. Her pictures were small in size, but detailed with good colourings.
Exhib. S.S. (7).

EVANS, — op. 1774
Exhib. F.S. (1), Game.

EVANS, — op. 1836
An uninitialled painter by whom was a 'Landscape and Dead Game' at the F.S. in this year.

*FAIRCLOTH, SHIREEN. b. East Sheen, Surrey 6th January 1936
For many years a fashion artist, turning to the painting of birds and animals in 1970 – now concentrates on drawing and painting animals and birds, and animal skeletons for books, advertising and encyclopedias. Exhibitor at the Society of Wild Life Artists; Chenil Gallery, Chelsea etc. Trained at the Sidcup School of Art.

FAUNER, H. op. 1834
London address.
Exhib. S.S. (1), Game.

*FENNESSY, RENA MARGARET, Mrs. (nee Gilmore). b. Southampton 26th February 1920
Started painting birds in 1960, and animals (specialisiing in the big cats) in 1962. Studied anatomy under Professor Reiner Hoffman. Spends much time each year in the field studying and sketching subjects and habitat. Designed a definitive set of Bird stamps for Uganda in 1964, followed by Animals for Kenya, Fish for Tanzania, Flowers for Uganda, Shells for Kenya and Butterflies for Tanzania, and many special commemorative sets for the three countries. Member Jersey Arts Group until 1920, also Kenya Arts Society until 1965. Bird paintings executed in water colours with some gouache. Resident in Nairobi, Kenya.
Exhib. First one-man show at New Stanley Art Gallery, Nairobi 1968, and another 1970. Game Coin Conference, San Antonio, Texas 1969. Tryon Gallery, London (Bird Artists of the World) Nov. 1972. Regular exhibitor at Tryon Gallery, Nairobi.
Repr. Limited edition of 6 Bird Paintings published by Tryon Gallery Ltd. London. Stamps for several African countries as noted above.

FENTON, ENOS. op. 1832-1860
Showed views and paintings of birds at the R.A. (1); B.I. (1); R.S.B.A. (5).

FERGUSON, WILLIAM GOUW. b. Scotland *c* 1632/33, d. *c* 1695
An early Scottish painter, who, following the custom of artistic compatriots, travelled abroad, to Italy and France, and finally to Holland, where he lived and worked so long that the Dutch claimed him as a national painter. He returned to England to die. His last known work is dated 1695. His works are almost entirely of dead birds and game, but always environed by landscape and architecture, much in the style of Jan Weenix (1621-1660) to whom they are usually attributed. These are skilful productions, carefully drawn and the impasto soft and fused, with a greyish hue, fine works of their peculiar class. Owing to the above-mentioned misattribution to Weenix, his works seem more rare than they actually are. He is better known abroad than in England, examples existing in the galleries of Berlin, Amsterdam and Hamburg. Two specimens are in the Glasgow Gallery and three in the National Gallery of Scotland (one dated 1684).
Auct. 'Mallord and their young and other water fowl' sold at Sotheby's in 1970.

*FERNELEY, JOHN E. b. Thrussington, Leicestershire 27th May 1782, d. Melton Mowbray 3rd June, 1860
Son of William and Ann Ferneley, being the youngest of six children of a wheelwright. In 1803 decided to be an artist and was encouraged by the Duke of Rutland. He is first and foremost a sporting painter. In Dover in 1804 painting the Officers of the Garrison. Left Dover in 1805 and joined Ben Marshall. Painted for Assheton Smith, the Master of the Quorn. We illustrate a 'Duck and Drake in a Landscape' S&D 1850, showing an example of his bird painting.

Lit. *Dictionary of British Sporting Painters* Paviére p. 38.
Coll. Harris Museum & A.G., Preston, 'Fox and Wild Duck'.

FERNELEY, Miss S. op. 1829
Exhib. S.S. (1), Game Birds.

FIELDER, — op. 1817
An uninitialled painter who exhibited a painting of a dead bird at the R.A. in this year.

FIELDING, NEWTON LIMBIRD SMITH. b. Durham 1799, d. Paris 1856
Youngest son of Nathan Theodore Fielding (op. 1775-1814). He had a name for painting birds, also well-known as an engraver and lithographer. Mainly a water colourist but painted a few oils, chiefly views on the French coast, showing him proficient in the medium, if somewhat hard in drawing and gaudy in colour. Had a considerable reputation in France, where he taught the family of King Louis Philippe.
Coll. V.&A., 'Ducks' S&D 1949.

FIELDING, Mrs. THEODORE HENRY ADOLPHUS (née Mary Anne Walton). op. 1815-1835
Wife of T.H.A. Fielding (b. 1781). Member of O.W.C.S. Painted flowers, birds and insects.
Exhibited as M.A. Walton from Manchester 1815-1819 at O.W.C.S. (14); then as Mrs. Fielding from London, B.I. (1); O.W.C.S. (31), Flowers and Birds.

FINLAYSON, Mrs. op. 1762-1768
Exhib. S.A. (1); F.S. (1), Birds.

FITZGEORGE, Mrs. PAULINE CELIA. b. Chadrington, Oxon.
Daughter of Sir James Gunn, R.A., the celebrated portrait painter. Her bird paintings are drawn on scraper-board and are coloured with a special process developed by the artist. She has been working on this method for over ten years but has never exhibited until the following.
Exhib. The Fox Sporting Gallery, Hale Park, Fordingbridge, Hants. (Nov./Dec. 1973).
Repr. *Country Life* (November 22nd 1973) advertisement.

FORSTER, GEORGE. op. 1772
An amateur, who showed a painting of birds at the R.A. in this year.

FOSTER, WILLIAM JOHN. op. 1885
Exhib. G.G. (1).

FRANCIS, Miss M. op. 1852
Exhib. S.S. (1), Game.

FROHAWK, F.W. (19th Century)
Repr. Bulter, A.G. 1896-8 *British Birds with their Nests and Eggs.*

FULLERTON, LEONARD. b. Aberdeen 1909, d. Newport-on-Tay 1968
After leaving school moved to Dundee, where he worked as an illustrator in the 'Courier' offices. Upon his marriage removed to Newport-on-Tay where he settled for the rest of his life. Began his career illustrating boys' stories and comic strips. Later he turned to painting in water-colours and gouache wild-life (mammals, birds etc) for which he is best known, these were reproduced on greeting cards, calendars and nature books. A deep knowledge of local natural history and concern with nature conservation made him much in demand as a speaker on the subject. Honorary Warden of Tentsmuir Point and Morton Lochs National Nature Reserve; President of Dundee Naturalists Societies.
Exhib. R.S.A.; Dundee City Museum & Art Galleries (Centenary exhib. 1873-1973); Glasgow Museums & Art Galleries (special exhib. 1974) his first one-man show.
Repr. Collins, Blackies, Valentines of Dundee Ltd, D. C. Thompson & Co, Jarrold Colour Publications, the 'Daily Record', etc.

GADSBY, W.H., R.B.A. op. 1891-1892
Painter of genre subjects, with the odd bird painting now and then.
Exhibited 'Chickens' at R.B.A. 1891 (No. 365) priced £80.

GARTLAN, KATHERINE MARY. b. Upton-by-Chester 23rd December 1946
Trained Chester School of Art, North Staffordshire Polytechnic, and Reading University. Paints in water colours, ink and conté. Many studies of birds made at Chester Zoo.
Exhib. S.W.L.A.

GAUDIER-BRZESKA, HENRI. b. near Orleans 1891, d. 5th June 1915
Mainly sculptor and draughtsman, influenced by Cubism and primitive art. Came to England on scholarships 1906 and 1908. Settled in Paris 1910 and married Sophie Brzeska. Came with her to London in 1911 using the combined name Gaudier-Brzeska. Had a studio in London. Founder member of the London Group 1913 and the Vorticists 1914-15. Joined French Army and was killed 1915.
Coll. The Tate Gallery possess several studies of birds and animals. Kettles Yard, Cambridge.

*GAYLARD, MARJORIE ORPIN, N.D.D., F.R.S.A. b. Newport (Mon.) 24th January 1925
Member S.W.L.A., painting in water-colour, oil, gouache, etc. Trained at Newport School of Art, Cordwainers Technical College, Central School of Arts & Crafts, London, West of England College of Art, also studied in France, Austria and Italy. Lecturer, Newport College of Art, also Designer of leather goods and printed textiles.
Exhib. Mall Galleries, London; Royal West of England Academy; Arts Council exhibitions; Birdland Art Gallery etc.

*GEE, ARTHUR. b. Latchford, nr. Warrington 10th January 1934
Self-taught artist specialising in wildfowl, waders and game birds, with emphasis on 'atmosphere' in his works. Member S.W.L.A.
Exhib. The Mall Galleries, McDonald Booth Gallery, Moorland Gallery, The Wildfowl Trust, Warrington Art Gallery.

GILES, JAMES. b. 1718, d. 1780
Of Huguenot stock. China and enamel painter with an address in Berwick Street, Soho. Decorated a great deal of Worcester porcelain. Thought to have been responsible for the noted *Dishevelled Birds* found on the wares from several English Porcelain Factories.
Lit. Worcester Porcelain by F. S. Mackenna (Lewis Publishers 1950).

GILLARD, W. active Liverpool 1850
Coll. 'Dead Game' and 'Spaniel with Dead Game' (Harris Museum & A.G., Preston).

*GILLMOR, ROBERT ALLEN FITZWILLIAM. b. Reading 6th July 1936
Birds and painting have been the principal interests of Robert Gillmor from boyhood. After studying in the Fine Art Department of Reading University he returned in 1959 to his old school, Leighton Park, as Director of Arts and Crafts – where he remained for six years, before turning to wildlife art as a full-time occupation. Since this time he has illustrated more than 50 books, specialising in pen-and-ink drawings, and in illustrating the habits and behaviour of birds. He is a founder-member and the Honorary Secretary of the Society of Wildlife Artists, and in addition is a Vice-President of the British Trust for Ornithology, and has served on the Councils of both the Royal Society for the Protection of Birds, and the British Ornithologists' Union. He is President of both the Reading Ornithological Club and the Cape Clear Bird Observatory.
Robert Gillmor is a great believer in the importance of studying the living bird, and has done plenty of sketching in the field, both in Britain and on expeditions to Iceland and trips to East Africa and the U.S.A. In both his prints and his water-colour paintings he is concerned with the design and composition of birds in their surroundings. His favourite bird groups are the waterside and sea birds particularly members of the heron family, waders and wildfowl.
Mediums. Water-colour, lino cuts, pen and ink.

Exhib. Boston, U.S.A., Reading Museum & A.G., Tryon Gallery, Nairobi (all one-man shows). Society exhibitions throughout Britain.
Coll. Ulster Museum; Reading A.G.; Curtis Museum, Alton; Laboratory of Ornithology, Cornell, New York.

GRAY, Miss K. op. 1873-1875
Exhib. R.A. (1); S.S. (3), Birds.

GREEN, ROLAND, F.Z.S. b. Rainham, Kent 9th January 1896, d. Hickling, Norfolk 1971
This well-known bird painter was primarily a water-colourist. He lived at Hickling on the Norfolk Broads for almost 50 years. His studio was beside Hickling Broad. He favoured the Broads for his work, but did visit Europe to study birds, and climbed the Cairngorms to sketch Golden Eagles. Illustrator of many bird books. Executed a large frieze in oils for Lord Desborough's shooting lodge. His father was a taxidermist and worked for a time at the Natural History Museum in London. He was unmarried.
Exhib. Frequent one-man shows at Ackermann's Galleries, Bond Street, London.
Repr. Author and illustrator of *Wing Tips*; *Birds in Flight* etc.

GREENWOOD, TIMOTHY JOHN
Exhib. S.W.L.A. 'Sparrowhawk', 'Short-eared Owl', 'Tengmalns Owl (Norway)', and 'Young Golden Eagle'.

GRIERSON, C. MACIVOR, R.I. op. 1874
Exhib. S.S. (1), Game.

*GRIFFIER, ROBERT. b. London 1688, d. *c* 1750
Elder son of Old Griffier – the younger being John (*c* 1690-1750) Junior. The history of the Griffiers is as much involved as the identification of their several products – mainly landscape paintings. Robert, like his father, was partial to river and marine pieces, but he did paint birds in romantic settings.
Lit. Grant *The Old English Landscape Painters,* vol. 1, p. 65.

GRISET, ERNEST HENRY. b. 1844, d. 22nd March 1907
Although of French birth he came to London in the 1860's and established himself. Illustrated books for the Dalziel brothers and made drawings for *Punch* and *Fun.* Exhibited drawings of animals at Suffolk Street in 1871.
Coll. V. & A. 'An Owl'.
Exhib. At S.S. in 1871 (from London address); at Chilham Antiques Ltd., near Canterbury, a pair of studies in oils of Golden Eagle and Harp Eagle.

GUERIN, Mrs. WILLIAM COLLINGS LUKIS DE (formerly Miss Anna Maria Edmonds). op. 1875-1885
London and Folkestone addresses. Exhibited at the Royal Academy 1875, Partridges, but her exhibits 1876-1880 were flowers.

GUNTON, W. op. 1829
London address.
In this year he exhibited three paintings of game birds at the R.S.B.A. He also painted dogs with his birds of sport.

HALL, Mrs. PAULINE SOPHIE, B.Sc. b. Birmingham 23rd June 1918
Member S.W.L.A. Art training at Michaelis School of Fine Art, Cape Town and Birmingham University (Zoology). Widow of Professor K. R. L. Hall, animal behaviourist and ornithologist. Mediums: wood-cuts, lino-cuts and wood engravings.
Exhib. Society of Painter-Etchers & Engravers, London. Royal West of England Academy. S.W.L.A. South African Association of Arts, Cape Town. Stellenbosch Museum, C.P., S. Africa.
Coll. Ulster Museum, Belfast. Ruskin Gallery, Stratford-on-Avon.

*HAMILTON, CARL WILHELM DE (or Charles William). 1668-1754
Despite his Dutch-sounding name he was in fact of Scottish descent, but went to Holland and assumed a Dutch name. The Sladmore Gallery, London, exhibited 'Pheasants in a Landscape' in December 1972 (see illustration). See also entry for James Hamilton, father of Charles William.

HAMILTON, JAMES. op. *c*1645, d. *c*1705
Born a Scotsman of Fifeshire, he fled to Brussels at the Revolution and founded there the family which practically ceased to be British, and are even designated as *von* or *de* Hamilton in foreign collections. He was chiefly a painter of birds and fruit.

HAMLYN, JANE T. op 1819
Exhib. R.A. (1), Game.

HANCOCK, JOHN. op. 1804, d. 1839
Painter of flowers, fruit, birds, figures and armorial bearings. At the Derby Porcelain Manufactory before 1823 until 1836, leaving the factory to design textiles in Lancashire.
Lit. *Crown Derby Porcelain* Gilhespy.

HANCOCK, JOHN THE ELDER. b. 1777, d. 1840
Painted birds in the Sevres style and flowers at the Derby Porcelain Manufactory about 1820. Worked with his brother George at Edward's Porcelain Factory at Burton-on-Trent *c*1839.
Lit. *Crown Derby Porcelain* Gilhespy; Chaffers.

HARDCASTLE, MISS CHARLOTTE. op. 1852-1866
London address. Royal Academy exhibits in 1855 (Snipes); in 1856 (Pheasants); 1864 (Teal), and in 1866 (A Plover).
Exhib. R.A. (9); B.I. (4); S.S. (12).

HARDY, HEYWOOD, A.R.W.S., R.E. op. 1861-1903
An animal and sporting painter, but like his brother James, Junior, he was apparently interested in birds – a 'Head of an Adjutant Bird' S&D 1874 is in the collection of the V. & A. Museum.

HARDY, JAMES, Junior. b. 1832, d. 4th April 1889
Not strictly a bird painter, but he does deserve a mention here as he is known chiefly for his paintings of dogs with game birds. Son of James Hardy, Senior (1801-1879) of Bath and a brother of Heywood Hardy (q.v.).
Coll. V. & A. Museum (1), Game.

HARTE, DENNIS F. (living)
Exhib. S.W.L.A., 'Kingfisher', 'Young Magpie', 'Purple Herons'.

HARRISON, J.C. b. Tidworth, Wilts 1898
As a young man studied and sketched birds, learning anatomy from the practise of taxidermy. Studied at Slade School after the 1914-18 war. Visited Scotland regularly and observed Golden Eagles at their eyrie, from a hide. As a result illustrated Seton Gordon's *Days with the Golden Eagle.* In 1938 went to Iceland to study the bird life and landscape. Wrote and illustrated *Bird Portraits* and illustrated Jean Delacour's *Pheasants of the World.* Toured Africa observing birds, animals and landscape. Lived for many years in Norfolk where he painted the rare birds of the Broads and also game birds in their natural surroundings.
Exhib. Tryon Gallery, London.

HAUGHTON, MOSES. b. Wednesbury 1734, d. Ashted, Nr. Birmingham 1804
Worked as a decorator of papier-mâché goods in Henry Clay's factory in Birmingham. Painter of still life, chiefly in water-colours; also designed and engraved Bible illustrations. Exhibited 13 portraits, paintings of dead game and subject pictures at the R.A. 1788-1804.
Coll. Birmingham Art Gallery 'An Owl' oil on panel.

HAWKINS, WATERHOUSE. op. 1832-1841
London address. Painted game birds, fish, etc. His R.A. exhibit in 1939 was 'Wounded Pheasant' and in 1840 'A Flemish Pheasant'.
Exhib. R.A. (5); B.I. (4); S.S. (16); N.W.C.S. (1).

HAYES, WILLIAM. (18th Century)
Painted birds. Published *Natural History of British Birds* (1775) and *Rare Birds in Osterley Park* (1794). Some drawings of birds hang in Mapperton House, the home of Viscount Hinchingbrooke. They were made for the 4th Earl of Sandwich, under whose patronage Hayes brought out his *Portraits of British and Exotic Birds* (1778). An inscribed copy of this work with original coloured drawings bound up in it is in Lord Hinchingbrooke's possession.
Coll. Lord Hinchingbrooke; J. C. Quilter.

HAYWOOD, JOHN.
Address in Warwickshire, near Coventry. A practising falconer of twenty years standing, owning a Goshawk, a Lugger Falcon and a Kestrel. In the last few years has taken to painting portraits of these fine birds. His latest collection of works being exhibited in London (June/July 1974).

HEARLIN, — op. 1765.
Exhib. S.A. (1), Game Birds.

HEFELE, — op. *c* 1690
Recorded by Walpole as painting landscape in water-colour, also birds and insects.

HENNESSEY, FRANK CHARLES. op. 1921-1926
A 'Crows in Spring' and a 'Gulls' sold at Christie's 2nd May 1973.

HENRY, MORRISON REID. b. Kandapola, Ceylon (now Sri Lanka) 17th February 1891
Member Society of Wild Life Artists exhibiting at the Society's exhibitions. A self-taught artist painting in tempera and oils. From 1911 to 1946 Systematic Entomologist to the Ceylon Government, Colombo Museum, Ceylon.
Exhib. S.W.L.A., Reading A.G., Arun Art Centre, Tryon Gallery, Sladmore Gallery. Also in Salisbury and Bulawayo, Rhodesia.
Repr. Author and illustrator of *Coloured Plates of the Birds of Ceylon,* 1927-1935, (64 plates published by the Ceylon Government). *A Guide to the Birds of Ceylon* 1955 & 1970, O.U.P.; also illustrated *Indian Hill Birds* by Salin Ali, O.U.P. 1949. Contributed 6 colour plates to *Handbook of the Birds of India and Pakistan* 1968/69, O.U.P.

HICKIN, GEORGE. op. 1858-1877
Greenwich address. His R.A. exhibits included 'A Mallard and Snipe' 1858; 'Dead Game' 1859, and 'Wild Ducks' 1862.
Exhib. R.A. (70); B.I. (6); S.S. (24); V.E. (26).
Coll. V. & A., Cochin China Fowls.

HICKS, Miss MARY. op. 1890
Exhib. S.S. (1), Game.

HILL, ROBIN. b. Brisbane 1932
Came to England at age of two, returning when 17.
Attended National Gallery of Art School, Melbourne. In 1962 covered 6,000 miles through the inland and tropical north of Australia, studying and sketching birds and wild life.
Exhib. The Tryon Gallery, London 1963, (Bird Artists of the World).
Illus. *Bushland & Seashore.*

HODGSON, R. op. 1780-1787
A painting of a Fighting Cock was in the Hutchinson collection, its present whereabouts unknown.

HOLD, ABEL. op. 1849-1871
A skilful painter of game, who exhibited 16 works at the R.A., 1 at the B.I., and 1 at the R.S.B.A. His exhibited works included 'Black Grouse, Woodcock and Snipes', 'Study of Game and Dogs', 'Red Grouse, Mallard, Woodcock', 'Pheasants, Hare, Partridge, etc.', 'High bred Pheasants, Woodcock and Hare', 'Red Grouse, Ducks and Snipes'.
Exhib. R.A. (16); B.I. (1); S.S. (1).

HOULDITCH, J. op. 1784-1791
A painter of game birds of which he exhibited specimens at the R.A.

HUDSON, A. M. op. 1829-1831
Exhib. S.S. (4), Birds.

HUDSON, Miss ANNE. op. 1830
Exhib. S.S. (2), Birds.

HUGGINS, Miss ANNA. op. 1854-1855
Exhib. R.A. (3), Game.

*HUGGINS, WILLIAM. b. 1820, d. 1884
Generally regarded as a painter of lions, tigers and other cats, but he did produce some bird subjects, mainly chickens, thus finds a place here.
Exhib. R.A. (31); B.I. (8).

HUGHES, WILLIAM. b. 1842, d. 1904
Son of Sir Herbert Hughes-Stanton and pupil of George Lance and W. H. Hunt. His main claim to fame are five large bird paintings made for the entrance hall of Lord Calthorpe's London House in Grosvenor Square. Mainly a still-life painter.
Exhib. R.A., B.I., S.S. and G.G.

HUMPHREYS, Mrs. HILDA FLORENCE. b. London 1911
Resident in East Barnet. Her work with birds is primarily modelling and sculpture, mostly stoneware pottery, figures and animals. Her paintings in oil, water-colour and line and wash, cover a variety of subjects including birds. Trained at Hornsey Art College and Central School of Arts & Crafts, London.
Coll. Luton Museum; Broomfield Park Museum, Southgate.
Exhib. R.A., S.W.L.A., and various smaller exhibitions.

*HUNT, EDGAR. op. 1873-1955
Son of Walter Hunt, Junior, painter of birds, animals and fruit pieces. His compositions were mostly farmyard scenes in which domestic poultry and their broods predominated. He worked in a meticulous manner – every feather painted to the minutest detail. Of a retiring disposition, seldom exhibiting, and living among the animals he owned and used as his models. His work became very popular even though he exhibited seldom.

JACKSON, G. op. 1844
Exhib. R.A. (1), Game.

JOHNSON, F. op. 1791-1797
Croydon address.
Exhib. R.A. (1) 'Snipes'; S.A. (3).

JOHNSON, ROBERT. b. Shotley, Northumberland 1770, d. Kenmore, Perthshire 1796
An engraver. Made water-colours for some of the wood-engravings for Bewick's *British Birds.* Apprenticed to Bewick.

JOHNSON, W., Junior. op. 1800-1809
Exhib. R.A. (2), Game.

KEARNS, ANN. b. Hull, E. Yorks 25th January 1934
Resident in Sevenoaks, Kent. Member of the Guild of Kent Artists. Keenly interested in all wildlife as a naturalist. Art training at Regional College of Art, Hull. Works in water-colours, pastel, wash and line. Also paints buildings in landscape and genre.
Exhib. Society of Wild Life Artists, Art Exhibitions Bureau and various other Galleries.

*KELLY, CHLOE ELIZABETH TALBOT. b. Hampstead, London 15th July 1927
Member Society of Wild Life Artists and Society Industrial Artists & Designers. Regular exhibitor at the F.B.A. Galleries, also shows at the Tryon Gallery, London. Almost entirely water-colour gouache. Self-taught but had father (R. B. Talbot Kelly) as critic and adviser.

KELLY, RICHARD BARRETT TALBOT, R. I. b. Birkenhead 20th August 1896, d. 30th March 1971
Used to exhibit regularly at R.A., R.I., S.W.L.A. and local provincial galleries. One-man exhibition at The Fine Art Society, London. Primarily a water-colour painter, but also painted in oils and poster-colour. Made models in wood, paper, clay, bronze, including some for the Festival of Britain. Art Master at Rugby School 1929-1966. Self-taught but with an artist for a father.Illustrated several books.
Coll. Birkenhead.

KERR, DAVID ORD.
Exhib. Sladmore Gallery, London 1973, 11 bird paintings of 11 different species.

KEYL, FRIEDRICK WILHELM. b. 1823, d. 1871
Of German origin, pupil and assistant to Landseer, and was patronised by Queen Victoria, painting portraits of animals on the Royal farms. With delicate care he inserted ducks and song birds in the settings of his portraits of cattle.
Exhib. R.A. (42); B.I. (34).

KIDD, JOSEPH BARTHOLOMEW. op. 1833-1858
Pupil of Rev. J. Thomson (q.v.). Member of the Scottish Academy of Painting, made the engravings for *The Miscellany of Natural History* with text by Sir William Jardine, Bt., F.R.S.A., F.L.S.

KILLINGBECK, BENJAMIN. op. 1769-1796
Thought to have been born in Leeds, beginning as a portrait painter. Commissions by Lord Rockingham and other noblemen to paint portraits of their horses. He produced also pictures of birds and sporting scenes.
Exhib. R.A. (11), all animals and birds; S.A. (12); F.S. (28).

KING, KATHERINE, Miss. op. 1869
London address. Painted game.

KNYFF, LEONARD. b. Haarlem 10th August 1650, d. London 1721
Apart from paintings of gentlemen's seats, he is also recorded as a painter of fowls and dogs. His 'Black-game and Rabbits with Swallows' is more spacious than the crowded compositions of his contemporary Francis Barlow.
Coll. Leeds A.G.

KOSTER, DAVID. b. London 1926
Founder member Society of Wild Life Artists. Mainly producing lithographic prints, but also paints in water-colour and oils. Lived many years in Scottish Highlands equipping a cottage for print production to which he returns annually. Keen naturalist apart from his specialist interest in birds and the proximity of sea and mountains and the bird life providing stimulus. Frequents also the London Zoo for his special bird subjects, Pheasants and Owls. Trained at Slade School, now teaches at Medway College of Design.
Exhib. S.W.L.A., R.A. and numerous Galleries through the country.
Coll. Works in the Art Galleries of Aberdeen, Belfast, Oldham, Hull, Southampton, Coventry, Bolton, Ministry of Public Works, many Education Authorities, Shipping companies and Industrial undertakings.
Repr. Mural for Royal Veterinary College, London; R.S.P.B. Magazine (cover).

KOZANECKI, L. op. 1839-1848
Exhib. R.A. (3), Game.

*LACEY, Mrs. MARY ELLIOT, A.T.D., S.W.L.A. b. Birmingham 26th September 1923
Founder member of the Society of Wild Life Artists, exhibiting at the Mall Galleries annually. Has also exhibited in America, Luxembourg and Jersey. Trained at the Birmingham College of Art. Works in water-colours, oils, conté and pencil. Regular exhibitor with the Frances Iles Gallery, Rochester; Brotherton Gallery, Beaminster; Ashbarn Gallery, Petersfield; Birdland Art Gallery, Bourton-on-the-water, and holds a one-man show annually in Croydon.
Repr. Series of Butterfly paintings for Hamlyn's *Prints for Pleasure* and illustrations for Hamlyn's *Junior Encyclopedia of Wildlife.*

LAMBERT, E.F. op. 1823-1846
London address. His R.A. exhibit 1827 was 'Pheasants'.
Exhib. RA. (15); S.S. (7).

LAYTON, F.W. op. 1873
Exhib. S.S. (3), Game.

*LEAR, EDWARD. b. Holloway 12th May 1812, d. San Remo 29th January 1888
His artistic achievements were many and extremely varied. He contributed to many works. A much-travelled artist, there was hardly a portion of Europe to which he had not been, while not neglecting his native England. In 1832 Lear was asked by Lord Stanley, heir to the Earl of Derby, to come and stay at Knowsley, and draw the animals and birds in his private zoo. This resulted in a volume of 108 water-colour drawings dating from 1832 to 1837. The son of Jeremiah Lear, a London stockbroker, and twentieth in a family of twenty-one.
Exhib. Edward Lear 1812-1888. A loan exhibition Oct./Nov. 1968 by Gooden & Fox Ltd., Bury Street, London. Included a Red and Yellow Macaw; Blue and Yellow Macaw; Sulphur and White Breasted Toucan; Common Crane; Common Swan; Black-tailed Gannet.
Rerp. *A Century of Birds from the Himalayan Mountains* John Gould 1832. *The Birds of Europe* John Gould 1837. *The Naturalists Library* Sir William Jardine 1843. *The Genera of Birds* G. R. Gray 1849. *The Family of Psittacidae, or Parrots* E. Lear 1832.

LEE, FREDERICK RICHARD, R.A. b. Barnstaple 1798, d. South Africa 1879
One time in the Army. Studied at the R.A. Schools. Painted landscapes, still life. His R.A. exhibits included in 1840 'Caper Caille, Blackcock, Grouse and Ptarmigan' and 'Deer and Heron'; in 1841 'Eagle and Blackcock in a Highland Glen'.
Exhib. R.A. (171); B.I. (131); S.S. (24).

LENGO, H. op. 1872
Exhib. S.S. (1), Birds.

LESLIE, G. op. 1832-1835
Exhib. R.A. (4); S.S. (4); N.W. (4), Game.

LEWIN, JOHN WILLIAM. 18th century
Brother of William Lewin. Engraved natural history subjects. Made the illustrations for *Birds of New Holland* etc.
Coll. B.M., Sydney A.G.

LEWIN, WILLIAM. op. 1789-1795
Brother of John William Lewin. Drew and engraved the plates for *Birds of Great Britain* 1795.

LIVENS, H.M. op. 1891-1892
Exhibited a 'Fowls' at the R.B.A. 1891-92.

LIZARS, WILLIAM. b. Edinburgh 1788, d. Edinburgh 1859
Received instruction from his father, an engraver, later in the Trustees Academy. He was a subject painter. On death of his father he devoted the remainder of his life to engraving. He engraved 222 plates of *British*

Ornithology after Selby. 2 volumes (Bohn) 1841. Also illustrated *The Naturalists Library* with text by Sir William Jardine. *c* 1833.
Auct. Christie's 8th May 1974 'British Ornithology' illus. Lizars 2 vols.

LOCK, A.H. op. 1874-1875
Exhib. V.E. (2), Birds.

*LODGE, GEORGE E. 1860-1954
Painter of birds and a falconer. A keen naturalist, friend of J. G. Millais and Archibald Thorburn. Studied and worked in London before moving to Camberley. Wrote and illustrated *Memoirs of an Artist Naturalist* and illustrated D. A. Bannerman's *The Birds of the British Isles*' 12 vols. 1953-63. Worked right up to his death at 93.
Exhib. R.A. (7); Tryon Gallery held an exhibition of his works in 1965, mostly birds of prey.

LONG, J. op. 1819
Exhib. R.A. (1), Game.

LUCAS, SAMUEL. b. Hitchin 1805, d. there 1870
Painted mills and shady lanes, also cattle and birds, with occasional sea pieces, sometimes on large canvases. North Wales was a favourite site with him.
Exhib. R.A. (7); B.I. (4); R.S.B.A. (2) both oil and water-colour.
Coll. B.M.

LUKER, Miss. op. 1868
London address.
Exhib. S.S. (1), Game.

LUKER, WILLIAM, Jnr. b. 1867, active 1885-1900
Painted landscape, genre, portraits and birds – being rather partial to the parrot family. He was also an illustrator. Exhibited at the R.A., S.S., N.W.C.S. and V.E.
Exhib. R.B.A. 1899 No. 57 'Forty-winks' a pair of Parakeets £10.10.0 1899/1900 No. 135 Parrots 'At top of the tree' £15.15.0. 1900 No. 299 'Macaw on a stand'.

LYNDEN. op. 1783
Painted flowers and birds.
Exhib. Free Society (4); Society of Artists (1).

MACDONALD, ALEXANDER, M.A. b. 1839, d. Oxford 16th October 1921
Appointed by Ruskin as the first Master of Drawing at Oxford University in 1871. Keeper of the University Galleries, 1882-1908. Painted still life, birds, landscapes and portraits.
Coll. Harris Museum & Art Gallery, Preston (Robin, w.c.).

MACDONALD, GEORGINA, (Lady Burne-Jones). b. 1840, d. 1920
Wife of the artist Sir Edward Burne-Jones whom she married in 1860 in Manchester.
Coll. Tate Gallery, London (Dead bird, w.c.).

*MARKS, HENRY STACY, R.A., R.W.S., R.E. b. London 13th September 1829, d. London 9th January 1898
Son of a coachbuilder, who employed him painting heraldic devices on carriages. Studied first at James Mathews Leigh's Art School, became a student at the Royal Academy in 1851, which he left to journey with Calderon to Paris, where he entered the Ecole des Beaux-Arts. Returned to England in 1853, exhibiting his first picture at the R.A. in that year. Elected A.R.A. in 1871, R.A. in 1878 and in 1896 an Honorary retired Academician. Associate of the O.W.C.S. in 1871 and a member in 1883. Was one of the founders of the 'St. John's Wood Clique'. He first confined himself to Shakespearean subjects, afterwards turning his attention to natural history, principally birds. His Studio sale was held at Christie's on 26th March 1898.
Exhib. R.A. (1853-1897, B.I., G.G., etc.
Coll. Walker A.G., Liverpool; V. & A. Museum (have number of his bird studies).

MARSHALL, BENJAMIN. 1767-1835
One of our most celebrated painters of Sport. Racing and hunting were his chief subjects, but he also depicted game-cock fighting, thus qualifying a place in this Dictionary. His accuracy and clarity, combined with pictorial treatment, rendered him in his day, and in this, perhaps the most valued of all painters in his special line. Working chiefly at Newmarket.

MARTELL, ISAAC. op. 1780-1788
Painter of game, live and dead, of fish, of fruit, of 'deceptions' and of landscapes.
Exhib. R.A. (9); S.A. (7).

MARTIN, T.W. op. 1847
London address.
Exhib. S.S. (2), Game.

MEDLAND, LILIAN. b. 1880, d. 1955
Four bird paintings by this artist were on show in a Sussex Dealer's premises in September 1973.
Exhib. Harrods' Picture Gallery, London, 30th May – 15th June 1974. One-man show of Bird Paintings.
Repr. *Country Life* 30 May 1974 p. 1376.

MEE, MARGARET URSULA (Mrs. R.B. Greville) b. Chesham 1909
S. Paulo, Brazil address. Studied in London at St. Martin's School of Art, Central School of Art and Camberwell School of Art. National Diploma in Painting and Design 1950. Resident in Brazil since 1952. Painter of flowers mostly but includes birds.
Coll. Hunt Botanical Library (4).
Exhib. Jardim Botanico, Rio de Janeiro; Royal Horticultural Society 1960 (awarded Grenfell Gold Medal); Tryon Gallery, London 1968.

MEIGH, Mrs. FRANCES EVELYN, A.R.C.A. b. London 1931
Works mainly in pastel. Lives in the country (Gloucestershire), has a waterfowl collection which forms the basis for study and inspiration. Also paints portraits. Studied Wimbledon School of Art and Royal College of Art.
Exhib. R.A., S.W.L.A., The London Group, Slimbridge Wildfowl Trust and Peakirk Wildfowl Trust.

MENCIE, M. op.1873
Exhib. S.S. (1), Birds.

MERRIN, PETER. b. Spondon, Derbyshire 1st August 1930
Designer, graphic artist and bird painter with the R.S.P.B. Illustrator of book relating to British wild birds and nature conservancy. Teacher of painting in water-colours, gouache and oils. Trained at Derby College of Art. Member Huntingdon Art Group. Also paints miniatures of wild life subjects, the smallest being about $1\frac{1}{2}$ inches square and painted with the use of a magnifying glass.
Exhib. R.S.P.B. and various provincial Galleries.
Coll. Derby A.G., Shuttleworth Collection.

MEYER, M. op. 1834
Exhib. R.A. (2), Game.

MILES, G. op. 1822-1824
Exhibited 3 paintings of game at the B.I.

MILLAIS, JOHN GUILLE. b. 1865, d. 1931
Son of Sir John Millais, P.R.A. An outstanding naturalist. George Lodge and Archibald Thorburn were among his friends.
Author of *The Natural History of British Game Birds* London (1909), and *The Natural History of British Surface Feeding Ducks* London (1902), both of which with illustrations after Thorburn and Millais.
Exhib. Fine Art Society, 1910 and 1921.

MOLE, Miss CLARA. op. 1886-1887
Exhib. N.S. (3), Birds.

MONAHAM, HUGH C.
Repr. Frost & Reed Ltd, Bristol, reproduced in colour *Greylag on the Loch; Mallard – Anglesey,* and *Sprigs in the Fall* by this artist.

MONGER, J. op. 1832-1845
Exhib. S.S. (7), Game.

MORLAND, JOHN. (living)
Repr. Several bird and flower prints by Glastonbury Prints.

MORR, J. op. 1854
Exhib. R.A. (1); S.S. (1), Game.

MORRIS, ALFRED. op. 1853-1873
Deptford address. Painted animals and game.
Exhib. R.A. (2) both landscapes; B.I. (17) and S.S. (14).

MORRIS, R. op. 1863
London address.
Exhib. S.S. (1), Game.

*MORTON, MICHAEL ROBERT. b. Delhi 18th March 1938
Almost entirely self-taught. Works in water-colour and gouache.
Exhib. Arun Art Centre, Arundel; Eastgate Gallery, Chichester; Goya Gallery, Christchurch, Hants.
Repr. R.S.P.B. Journal *Birds,* part illustrator *A World Atlas of Birds.*

MOTT, J. op. 1854
Exhib. R.A. (1); S.S. (1), Game.

MOTTRAM, J.M. op. 1888
Exhib. N.W.C.S. (1), Birds.

MULREADY, WILLIAM, Junior. b. London 1805, op. 1831-1842
Son of William Mulready, R.A. Painted game birds.
Exhib. R.A. (6); B.I. (7); S.S. (5), Game.

MURPHY, EDWARD HENRY, A.R.H.A. b. Dublin 1796, d. 1847
An Irish painter of birds and flowers. Committed suicide.
Exhib. R.H.A. 1826-1841.
Coll. National Gallery, Dublin.

MURPHY, PHILLIP ALAN. (living)
Exhib. S.W.L.A., 'Collared Dove'.

MUSGRAVE, THOMAS M. op. 1844-1862
Painter of game, exhibiting 2 works at the R.A., 8 at the B.I., 10 at the R.S.B.A.

MYN, ROBERT VAN DER. b. London 1724, living in 1764
One of a family of five painters who worked in England, all derived from Herman Van der Myn (Mijn) 1724 – op. 1764. All painted the same subjects, and much alike, fruit, flowers, portraits. Robert added game to the family repertoire, depicting birds of sport in a skilful manner and setting them in pretty landscape surroundings of a Scottish aspect. As he was actually born and buried in England, he takes his place as a native artist, and one of considerable charm in his line. He is last heard of in Lancashire, foregathering there with that county notability 'Tim Bobbin' (J. Collier, q.v.) in 1761.

NEALE, EDWARD. op. 1850-1910
This ornithologist and artist painted the wild birds and animals of the Scottish countryside.
Exhib. R.A. (1); B.I. (6) and S.S. (9).

NEVILLE, JANE PENN (Mrs. Repetto-Wright). b. Richmond, Yorks, 28th August 1949
Member Society of Wildlife Artists – painter of birds and mammals in water-colour, gouache and pen and ink. Trained at Loughborough College of Art as a textile designer of printed fabrics, gaining a Diploma in this subject.
Exhib. The Mall Galleries, London; Ashley Gallery, Shalbourne, Wilts.; Century Gallery, Henley, Oxon.

NICHOLAS, PAUL ALEXANDER. b. Stockton-on-Tees 13th January 1943
Self-taught artist painting in water colours and gouache. Was drawing wildlife (birds, reptiles etc.) at an early age with coloured crayons, starting water-colour when 12 years old. Interested in wildlife, photography, butterflies, wild flowers, the English countryside and birdwatching. Has had several one-man exhibitions n North East England.
Exhib. Shipley Art Gallery, Gateshead; Arundel Art Centre; Birdland Art Gallery, Bourton-on-the-Water, and Veryan Gallery, Cornwall.

NICHOLSON, RICHARD E. op. 1882-1888
Exhib. R.A. (2); N.W.C.S. (1), Birds.

NIEKERK, SARAH VAN. b. London 16th January 1934
Educated in America and at Bedales School. Art training at Central School of Arts & Crafts and Slade School of Fine Art, studied under Gertrude Hermes. Wood engraver and lino cut artist.
Exhib. R.A.; R.I.; Royal West of England Academy; Reading Museum; V. & A. London; Whitechapel Art Gallery; Welsh Arts Council; City A.G., Manchester; Glasgow, etc.
Coll. V. & A.; Reading; National Museum of Wales, etc.

NIXON, JOHN. op. 1781, d. 1818
A Merchant in the City of London, and probably, as an artist, an amateur, but he worked and exhibited consistently, becoming notable as a caricaturist of somewhat coarse humour. His social geniality made him an appropriate Secretary of the Beef Steak Club. Amongst his numerous farcical pieces were as many embodying views and landscape as in those of his congener Rowlandson, his probable model. These are usually places of fashion and resort – Bath, Brighton, Worthing – but some, e.g. in Devon, Wales and Ireland, are purely landscape with no intrusion of busy humanity. Several of his topographical views were engraved for Sandby's and other publications. That he painted birds is known, an 'Eagle Owls at Arundel Castle' S&D 1807 was sold at Christie's on 6th Navember 1973.
Exhib. R.A. (41).
Coll. V. & A. (9 drawings).

NODDER, R. P. op. 1786-1820
A not unknown painter of animals and birds, his work, scarce today, is sought for by connoisseurs of such pieces. He was probably related to, if not the same, as F. P. Nodder, a flower-painter and designer in human hair, a frequent fantasy in the 18th century, who worked from 1773-1788.
Exhib. R.A. (27).

NORTHCOTE, JAMES, R.A. b. 1746, d. 1831
This noted portrait and subject painter is entitled to some mention here by reason of the fine and little-known paintings of animals, birds and scenes of sport, including landscape, which he made as a side-line to his immense practice in other branches. A 'Teal' S &D1770 is known and is an example of his productions of this type.
Repr. Illustrated *Aesop's Fables* and exhibited a number of these at the B.I.

NOVICE, GEORGE W. op. 1824-1833
Painter of mixed subjects, including birds and landscapes of which he exhibited 3 at the R.A., 4 at the B.I., 5 at the R.S.B.A.

O'BRIEN, JOHN. (living)
Repr. Birds and animals as motifs on Silk Scarves specially designed for Rowland Ward.

OLIVER, ISAAC. op. 1824-1853
London address.
Exhib. S.S. (15), Game.

O'NEALE, JEFFERYES HAMETT. b. Ireland, d. 1801
In 1765 resident Adam & Eve Court, Oxford Road, London. 1770-1771 working for Wedgwood. Resident in Worcester 1768-1770. In London 1770 at the Chelsea Porcelain factory. Painted flowers, birds and landscapes.
Exhib. Free Society 1763-1772 (miniatures).
Lit. *Worcester Porcelain* Mackenna 1950.

OSTELL, Miss MARY M. op. 1893
Exhib. N.W.C.S. (1), Game.

PADDY, C. M.
Exhibited 'A feathered gathering' at R.S.B.A. 1891/2.

PAIGE, JOHN P. b. 1927
Main subjects natural history and railways. Fifteen years in the army followed by a year as a game-warden in Uganda: then trained at Lincoln School of Art and Birmingham College of Art & Design as a graphic designer: now free-lance.
Coll. Belfast Museum; Lincolnshire Arts Association (permanent collection).
Exhibits regularly with the Society of Wild Life Artists, also Wildfowl Trust exhibitions.
Illustrator of wild life subjects and children's books for Longmans.

*PAILLON, PETER. op. 1744-1784
Painter of birds and animals. Painted many birds from specimens collected by Joseph Banks in Newfoundland and Labrador. Often confused with Peter Paillon who lived in Islington and Glasgow and worked as a miniaturist; this is probably his son.
Coll. McGill University Library, Montreal; British Museum, London.
Exhib. S.A. 1778 (Horned Owl); R.A. (68); F.S. (1).
Repr. Pennant T. *British Zoology* 1766; Williams, pl. XXV; Lysaght, A.M. *Joseph Banks in Newfoundland & Labrador* 1766.
Lit. Williams.

PARKINSON, SYDNEY (or Sidney). b. Edinburgh 1745, d. 1771
Worked originally as a woollen draper, then turned to painting. Sailed with Cook and Joseph Banks on the *Endeavour* in 1768 and illustrated many of the birds found on that expedition. Died on the return voyage. Painter of birds, insects, animals and flowers.
Coll. British Museum; National Library, Canberra.
Exhib. Free Soc. 1765-6 (4).

PARRY, DAVID. b. 1942
Painter of birds and wildlife. Studied drawing, painting and illustration at Tunbridge Wells Art School and the Central School of Art, London. Illustrator of wildlife subjects and children's books for Longman's. Has travelled extensively. Works in oils and water colours.
Exhib. One-man show at Leslie & Peel Gallery, Brasted, Kent (June 1974).

PARRY, H. op. 1825
Exhib. S.S. (2), Dead Game.

PARSLOW, ROSEMARY. (living)
Illustrated *Breeding Birds of Britain & Ireland* John Parslow.

PARSONS, Mrs. GWENDOLENE FRANCES JOY. b. Manchester 9th July 1913
Member of Society of Wildlife Artists, London Society of Women Artists, and Scottish Society of Women Artists. Has exhibited at R.I., R.O.I., Pastel Society, R.S.M.A., etc. Mainly painter of flowers but includes wildlife in her repertoire, which includes birds, mostly in water-colour. Trained under Edward Swan, the late Jack Merriott and William Watkins. Recent work includes a 40 ft. mural for 'Birdland' at Bourton-on-the-Water, and a smaller mural comprising birds in variety and natural setting painted for a Swanage Hotel.
Coll. Russell Cotes Art Gallery, Bournemouth (mural for Wildlife showcase).

PARVIN, BETTY. b. Cardiff 1917.
Trained in sculpture, ceramics and life drawing at Nottingham College of Art. Studied water-colour painting under Basil Bastow. Unfortunately progressive damage to limbs by rheumatoid arthritis has resulted in a narrowing of artistic activity to bird watching and drawing of birds mainly as illustrations.
Exhib. Nottingham Society of Artists.

PASMORE, JOHN. op. 1830-1845
Painter of animals and birds.
Exhib. R.A. (11); B.I. (3); R.B.A. (3).

PASMORE, JOHN F. op. 1841-1866
Like the above, to whom he was probably related, he painted birds, also rural subject pictures and landscapes.
Exhib. R.A. (30); B.I. (23); R.B.A. (11).

PEARCE, DENNIS J. b. Yeovil, Somerset 21st August 1926
Trained as a technical illustrator working on Aircraft publications, self-taught as a wildlife artist, painting animals and birds. Member of the Society of Wildlife Artists, exhibiting annually from 1964, including the touring exhibitions through the British Isles. Also at Arun Art Gallery and Folkestone Art Gallery. First one-man show at Yeovil Museum (March 1973). Paints in gouache, oils and ink. Also book illustrator.
Repr. Animal studies by Medici Society, also Royle Publications Ltd.
Coll. Naval Air Command, R.N. Air Station (HMS 'Heron') Wardroom, Oil of a 'Heron'.

PEARSON, Mrs. JAMES, (née Eglington Margaret Paterson). op. 1775-1777, d. London 1823
Painter of birds and insects, often in landscape, exhibited 10 examples at the S.A. She was daughter of Samuel Paterson, a book auctioneer. Married James Pearson a noted glass-stainer (op. 1775, d. 1805).

PELLETIER, A. op. 1816-1847
Painter of birds and fruit, with an occasional landscape. He exhibited 32 works at the R.A. including 'Foreign Birds' (1822) and 'Gold Pheasant' (1830), also exhibited at O.W.C.S.

PEMBERTON-LONGMAN, JOANE, R.S.M.A. (deceased)
Exhib. S.W.L.A., 'Jays', 'The lost one'.

*PENFOLD, W.F. op.1870
A 'Ducks and Ducklings at water's edge' S&D 1870 was exhibited at the Galleries of Oscar & Peter Johnson Ltd. (Nov. 1973) (illustrated).

PETTY, ROBERT. b. London 1740, d. Holland 1789
Lived for a time in Hamburg. Painted flowers, fruit and birds in water-colour.

PIETERSEN, JACQUELINE. b. Londonderry, Ireland 24th May 1899
Founder member of the Society of Wildlife Artists. Trained at Beckenham School of Art and the Royal College of Art.
Exhib. Royal Academy, S.W.L.A., New English Art Club, Mall Galleries etc.

PIGEON, Mrs. op. 1772
Exhib. S.A. (1), Birds.

PITMAN, Miss JANETTA. op. 1880-1901
Painted genre, still life, flowers etc. Resident at Basford, Notts. Her exhibits included 'Dead Wood Pigeons'.
Exhib. R.A., S.S., B.I.

PITMAN, JOHN. op. 1820-1827
Worcester address.
Exhib. R.A. (1); B.I. (1); S.S. (1), Game.

PITT, R. op. 1795
London address. He sent a painting of a 'Kingfisher' to the R.A. in this year.

PLACE, FRANCIS. b. Yorkshire 1647, d. York 1728
Younger son of Rowland Place of Dinsdale. Placed with a Solicitor in London until 1665 when he left owing to the plague. He painted, designed, etched and engraved in mezzotint and painted portraits and landscape. Refused a pension of £500 a year offered to him in the reign of Charles II to illustrate for the Navy. His widow disposed of his paintings, some of fowlers, fowl and fish. Etched plates of birds after Barlow.
Coll. Harris Museum & A.G., (etchings after Barlow).

POULTON, JAMES. op. 1844-1859
His R.A. Exhibits included 'Pigeons' (1844), 'Game' (1859). Brother of the landscapist George P.
Exhib. R.A., B.I. and S.S.

PRATT, DAVID ELLIS, M.S.I.A., F.Z.S. b. Kobe, Japan 21st June 1911 (living)
Founder member of the Society of Wildlife Artists. Exhibiting mostly at the Federation of British Artists. Painting in oil, water-colour and usual mediums. Illustrator for scientific publications and popular natural history books, and periodicals for children.
Lit. *Animal Kingdom* by S. Money with 400 illustrations, (Hamlyn).

PRESTON, JOSEPHINE. op. 1888
Exhib. S.S. (1), Birds.

PUTMAN, DAVID.
Exhib. S.W.L.A., 'Widgeon grazing', 'Widgeon at Rest'.

PYBUS, H. op. 1839
In this year he sent four pictures of game-birds to the R.S.B.A.

QUARTREMAINE, G.W. op.1881-1882
Stratford-on-Avon address.
Exhib. V.E. (2), Game Birds.

RANDALL, JOHN. fl. 1826
Painted birds at Coalport and Madeley China Manufactories.

RANDLE, FLORENCE. op. 1879-1880
Exhib. V.E. (2), Birds.

RANKIN, GEORGE.
A 'Grouse Flying' auctioned at Sotheby's (11th May 1966).

*RAWLING, BRIAN. b. Wharfedale, Yorkshire 1928
This gifted Yorkshire-born artists paints birds, mammals (especially Deer) and sporting scenes with equal facility in water-colour. His bird pictures are mainly concerned with game birds and wildfowl, with which he has had long experience as a sportsman. For many years he has bred pheasants both for ornamental purposes and for sporting purposes and has thus had close contact with this species. Rawlings is also widely known for his deer paintings.
Exhib. The Macdonald Booth Gallery, London on several occasions.

READ, JOHN. op. 1773-1783
Bedford address.
Exhib. S.A. (31); R.A. (2), Game.

REED, BRYAN. b. 1934
His early work was as a graphic designer and illustrator. Spent two years in Egypt with the R.A.F. where he spent considerable time painting desert landscapes and developing his superb miniaturist technique. A development from this was an exhibition of surrealist paintings held in Sussex in 1966. He then moved to Norfolk and began painting birds, holding a successful one-man show there in 1969. A full-time painter, he works from field sketches and technical details taken from skins.
Exhib. Sladmore Gallery, London 1973 in 'Bird Artists of Today', and in 1972 combined with Richard Weatherly in a two-man show at the same Gallery.

REID-HENRY, DAVID. b. Ceylon 1919
Son of George Henry, the author and illustrator of many ornithological works. Educated in England and spent two years in the City prior to entering the army at outbreak of the 1939 War. Whilst at Sandhurst he was able to spend much of his spare time in the studio of George Lodge whose tradition he inherits and who gave him invaluable encouragement. His army service took him to North Africa with a Tank Regiment and later he commanded a unit in Ceylon. Since the war he has lived in Africa for a considerable period and many of his paintings were executed and planned there. His interests include falconry, shooting and cricket.
Exhib. The Sladmore Gallery, London.
Repr. *The Eagles, Hawks & Falcons of the World* by Amadon & Brown.

*REINAGLE, PHILIP, R.A. 1749-1833
Of Hungarian origin, his family emigrating to England in 1745 as adherents to the young Pretender. He therefore learned his art in Scotland under Allan Ramsay, coming to London in 1796. That art was so various as to defy definition, Reinagle being equally adept and industrious in portrait, animals, still life, birds and landscape, a bold and masterly hand apparent in all, especially perhaps in birds, of which a life-size 'Eagle' is a masterpiece of fierce energy. Philip Reinagle's output was immense, an oeuvre exceeded only by his son, Ramsey.
Coll. Sir Maurice Bromley-Wilson, Bt., (Partridge & chicks.
Exhib. R.A. (114); B.I. (138); R.B.A. (1).

REVILL, W. H. op. 1868-1870
Exhib. S.S. (5), Poultry.

RICHARDS, W. op. 1838-1841
Exhib. S.S. (3), Game.

RICHTER, M. op. 1851
Exhib. R.A. (2), Game.

*RICKMAN, PHILIP CHARLES. b. Richmond, Surrey 1891
Resident in Sussex. Was taught drawing as a boy at his preparatory school. Later a pupil of the late George Lodge and a friend of Archibald Thorburn. One of the best of the bird painters of Britain today. Has had twenty-seven one-man exhibitions in London.
Exhib. Tryon Gallery, London and The Moorland Gallery, London.
Coll. The Glebow Foundation, Calgary, Canada; The Bentley collection; The Marlen collection, etc.
Repr. *Game Birds; Gun Room Guide* and wrote and illustrated *A Bird Painter's Sketch Book* and *Bird Sketches.*

RISDON, BETTY (Mrs. Elizabeth Sadler Risdon). b. Birmingham
Paints in Cryla. Art training includes short courses with Dr. Eric Ennion and at Rode Art Club held at The Tropical Bird Gardens near Bath. Has done a lot of research on illustrated Zoo Labels, some are to be seen

at the The Wildfowl Trust, Pointe-a-Pierre, Trinidad. Director of The Tropical Bird Gardens, Rode, near Bath.
Exhib. S.W.L.A. annual exhibition. Somerset Society of Artists, Bath and Taunton. Bath Society of Artists.

ROBERTS, SAMUEL. op. 1778-1824
London address. Exhibited at the Royal Academy (4), Still Life, Fish, Hares and Mallards.

ROBINSON, Miss G. op. 1879
Exhib. R.A. (13); V.E. (1), Birds.

*ROE, GEORGE. b. Newmarket, Suffolk 1930
A living water-colour artist of considerable talent, having spent two years at Cambridge Art school, two years at Hornsey College of Art and a similar period at St Alban's School of Art. Specialises in British Birds of most species, working on both small and large-scale pictures and is particularly happy with woodland birds and waders. He has developed the ability to suggest accuracy of plumage without overdoing the detail and thus losing the liveliness of his subjects. Now resident in Hertfordshire.
Exhib. The Macdonald Booth Gallery, London.

ROE, ROBERT HENRY. 1793-1880
He resided chiefly in Scotland, painting there the scenery and sporting incidents, with careful delineation of animals and birds. Later he worked both in London and Cambridge, at which last he was probably connected with an art business then well-known in the town.
Exhib. R.A. (10); B.I. (11); R.B.A. (16).

ROLFE, ALEXANDER F. op. 1839-1871
London address. There are four of this family, all painting in similar manner and subjects; fish, angling, sport and birds.
Exhib. S.S. and B.I.

ROLFE, Mrs. A.F. op. 1866
London address. Wife of Alexander R. Rolfe. Painted sporting subjects in the family tradition.
Exhib. S.S. (1).

ROLFE, EDMUND. op. 1830-1847
Painted fish and birds.
Exhib. R.A. (1); B.I. (6); S.S. (5).

ROLFE, F. op. 1849-1853
London address. Known to have painted fish, but presumably he would have painted like the rest of the Rolfe's, so he is noted here.
Exhib. B.I. (2); S.S. (4).

*ROLFE, HENRY LEONIDAS. op. 1847-1881
The most prolific of the Rolfe family of painters. Best-known for his fish and angling subjects – it is apt to be overlooked that he was equally at home painting birds in their natural surroundings. The Trafalgar Galleries, London (Autumn exhibition – Nov./Dec. 1966) nos 44-47 were all bird paintings (woodcock and partridges).
Exhib. R.A. (16); B.I. (23); R.B.A. (92); V.E. (40).

ROLLE, E. op. 1830
Exhib. R.A. (1), Game.

ROSSITER, FRANCES A. op. 1858-1892
From 1866 onward exhibited bird paintings in water-colours entirely.
Exhib. S.S. (1), Birds; R.A.; B.I.; N.W.C.S.

RUBENSTEIN. op. 1760-1761
Exhib. S.A. (5), Game.

RUYCKEVELT, RONALD VAN.
Trained at Wimbledon School of Art and Royal College of Art. Began as Designer at Worcester Royal Porcelain Company in August 1953. His first modelling was his own series of the small American birds. Visited Florida and subsequent visits to U.S.A. making extensive studies of birds and game birds in particular for an entirely new series. Was closely associated with the productions of Dorothy Doughty.

SARTORIUS, Miss M. op. 1813
Member of the remarkable family of eight painters. Probably the daughter of John Nott Sartorius and resident with him. She exhibited only Birds at the B.I. in this year.

SCHOLDERER, OTTO. b. 1834, d. 1902
German, but spent 28 years in England from 1871-1899 painting mostly genre, still life, portraits and game.
Exhib. R.A. (40); S.S. (7); G.G. (2); V.E. (18), Game.

*SCOTT, Sir PETER MARKHAM, M.B.E., D.S.C. b. 14th September 1909
Son of Captain R. F. Scott, Arctic explorer, etc. Studied at the R.A. School. Director of Severn Wildfowl Trust, Slimbridge. Painter and illustrator of wild birds, etc. Author and illustrator of several books devoted to birds.
Exhib. R.A.; Ackermann's Galleries, London (one-man exhibitions) since 1933.

SELLETT, J. op. 1797
Exhib. R.A. (2), Game.

*SHACKLETON, KEITH, R.S.M.A., S.W.L.A. b. Weybridge, 16th January 1923
Vice-President, Royal Society of Marine Artists, Founder Member and Hon. Treasurer Society of Wildlife Artists and Chairman of Artists League of Great Britain. His wildlife field work includes visits to the Arctic and Antarctic Polar regions, the Atlantic, Indian and Pacific Oceans. Also to Europe, Africa, America, Asia and Australia. Resident in London. Paints in oil mostly. Educated Melbourne, Australia and Oundle, England.
Exhib. R.A., R.S.B.A., R.S.M.A., S.W.L.A., Tryon Gallery, London, and Kennedy Gallery, New York.
Coll. Birkenhead A.G., National Maritime Museum, Greenwich, R.S.M.A. Diploma collection and many private collections.

*SHIRLEY, Mrs. VALERIE LESLIE. b. Egypt
Educated in England and studied at the Heatherly School of Art. Lived in Upper Egypt (Minia) by the Nile, where a great variety of wildfowl from Eastern Europe wintered and these were studied at first hand. Evacuated from Egypt in the Suez crisis and now resident in England (Berkshire). Painter of birds as a profession since 1967. Both Moorland and Sladmore Galleries in London regularly show her work. Member of Society of Wildlife Artists.
Exhib. S.W.L.A., The Wildfowl Trust, Slimbridge and Peakirk, Oxford, Gloucester and Christchurch Galleries and the Galleries at Bourton-on-the-Water, Eastbourne, Woburn, Arundel, Henley, etc.
Illus. In *The Swans* by Sir Peter Scott and the Wildfowl Trust. Also cards produced by Royle's for the same source.

SHRAPNELL, E. S. op. 1860
Shirley address.
Exhib. S.S. (1), Game.

SIBLEY, CHARLES. op. 1826-1847
Painted game birds and waterfowl, together with portraits and genré.
Exhib. R.A. (10); B.I. (6); S.S. (8).

SILLETT, JAMES. 1764-1840
Citizen of Norwich, and a senior contemporary of John Crome. Although he became a member of the now famous Norwich Society, serving even as its President in 1815, he is scarcely to be counted as of that 'Norwich School' which contains some of the most valued names in our Landscape Art. Served a long apprentice-

ship at the R.A. Schools from 1781 to 1790. He painted chiefly flower, fruit and game, all but one of his 43 exhibits at the R.A. being of this nature. He painted mostly in water-colour.
Exhib. R.A. (43); S.S. (2); V.E. (4).
Repr. Grant, vol. 5, p. 367 and plate 182 (partridges & young).

*SIMPSON, CHARLES WALTER, R.I., R.S.M.A. b. Camberley, 8th May 1885, d. Alverton, Penzance 3rd October 1971
Son of Major-General Simpson, C.B. Sir John Millais, G.F. Watts and H.W.B. Davis gave the boy encouragement. Studied under Lucy Kemp-Welch, later stayed and worked with Sir Alfred Munnings at Swainsthorpe. His first large oil was hung in the R.A. and from then on was a regular exhibitor at the Royal Academy. Moved to Paris to study at l'Atelier Julien in 1910. Back to Cornwall, married the portrait painter Ruth Alison in 1913 and continued painting large decorative canvases of wild duck, curlew, gulls and other sea birds. Painted many pictures of the Derby, Grand National and other sports meetings.
Exhib. R.A., R.I., and V.E.; Paris Salon 1923 (Silver Medal); Paris Salon 1924 (Gold Medal); San Francisco 1915 (Gold Medal).
Coll. Newcastle, Doncaster, Blackpool, Derby, Bournemouth, Gateshead, Newport, Paisley, Christchurch, and Dunedin, N.Z., Art Galleries.
Lit. *The Fields of Home* (his autobiography).
Illus. *El Rodeo, Leicestershire & its Hunts, The Harboro Country, Trencher & Kennel, Animal & Bird Painting* and others.

SINGER, ARTHUR.
Illustrated *Birds of the World* by O. L. Austin and the *Hamlyn Guide to Birds of Britain and Europe.*

SMITH, EDWARD REGINALD ANDERSON. b. London 1903
Served in the Royal Navy 1916-1934, and again 1939-1945. Farming until 1963, and upon retirement started painting, since when his work has been fairly widely exhibited.
Exhib. S.W.L.A., Armed Forces Art Society, Sussex Artists Association, Arun Art Gallery, etc.

SMITH, WILLIAM. op. 1813-1859
A painter resident in turn in London, Shrewsbury, Newport and Ongar. Painted many sporting scenes, fish, dogs, horses and birds, with some plain landscape in Staffordshire and Shropshire.
Exhib. R.A. (32); B.I. (15).

SNAPE, MARTIN. op. 1874-1901
Gosport address. Painter of birds, animals and landscape.
Exhib. R.A., S.S., G.G., etc.

SOPER, EILEEN A. (living)
Author-illustrator of a number of books on wildlife including *When Badgers Wake, Wild Encounters, Wanderers of the Field, Wild Favour, Muntjac* and articles on wildlife in *Country Life,* etc. Trained under her father, the late George Soper. Member of S.W.L.A. and R.P.E. Mediums used: copper-plate engraving, chalk, pencil, oils and water-colours.
Exhib. R.A., R.S.A., Glasgow Institute of Fine Arts, Walker A.G., etc.
Coll. British Museum; Grundy A.G., Blackpool; National Gallery of Canada; Los Angeles Art Institute and many private collections.

SOUTHGATE, FRANK, R.B.A. b. Hunstanton 1872, killed in action 1916
His untimely death in action during the 1914-1918 war was a tragic loss to English art because his depiction of wildfowl both in flight and stationery contained all the feeling and movement that only a great artist could portray. He was a true wildfowler and often lived 'rough' in a small tent in the parts of Norfolk where he could live with the birds that he painted. He was well-known in East Anglia as a character and is still remembered by many friends in Norfolk.
Exhib. Mandell's Gallery, Norwich.

SPACKMAN, ISAAC. op. 1750, d. Islington 1771
Painter of birds, animals and flowers. Produced small embossed paintings of birds about 1754-1770. Somewhat in the style of Samuel Dixon.
Exhib. Walker Gallery, Liverpool (January 1951).

SPILSBURY, EDGAR ASHE. op. 1800-1828
An amateur painter of animals, wild and domestic, and birds. His paintings of lions, tigers and panthers, etc. are of exceptional merit, and are sometimes mistaken for those of G. Stubbs (q.v.). His birds are of like merit. He exhibited 21 works at the R.A., 10 at the B.I., some are canvases of size.

SPRANKLIN, JOHN R. b. Taunton 26th April 1916
Son of Ernest Spranklin, Architect and Art Master at Taunton School after 1914. Mother was also an artist. Has drawn birds since childhood but not professionally.
Exhib. S.W.L.A. Mall Galleries 1972 & 1973, also Birdland Art Gallery, Bourton-on-the-Water.

STANESBY, JOHN. b. 1796
Apprenticed at the Derby Porcelain Manufactory where he worked until 1810. Painted leaves and birds at the Derby works.

STENNET, R. op. 1803
A painter of Birds at Bath, of whom little is known.
Exhib. R.A. (1), Game.

STEVENS, GEORGE, R.B.A. op. 1810-1875
Painter of animals, birds and fruits, his works being numerous and valued by connoisseurs of those subjects. The bulk of his output was seen at the R.B.A. of which he was Treasurer in 1828 and President in 1833. His bird paintings included 'Snipes and Water-rail', 'Portrait of two favourite birds', 'A Virginian Nightingale', 'Wounded Woodcock', 'Heron and Bittern contesting over a fish', 'Peackock and wildfowl', 'Peregrin Falcon', 'Ptarmigan', 'Pheasants', 'Covey of Partridges', 'Grouse' and many dead game pictures.
Exhib. R.A. (22); B.I. (75); R.B.A. (246) chiefly drawings with a few sizeable oils.

STREET, Miss KATE. op. 1880-1902
London address. Painted birds and flowers.
Exhib. R.A., S.S., N.W.C.S.

STUBBS, GEORGE, A.R.A. 1724-1806
The remarkably fine painting of the 'Greenland Falcon' S & D 1780 in the Paul Mellon collection by this very famous animal painter ensures his mention here.

SUMPTER, H. op. 1816-1847
A painter solely of still life, fish, fruit and birds, but his landscape settings are often pretty and accomplished.
Exhib. R.A. (45); B.I. (19); S.S. (16); O.W.C.S. (2).

SUTTON, ELIZABETH.
Exhib. S.W.L.A. (Shelduck and young).

SWAINSON, WILLIAM. op. 1832-1888
Bird plates of great beauty appeared in his *Zoological Illustrations* 1832-1833. He also exhibited a number of miniatures.

TARGETT, THOMAS G. op. 1869
Salisbury address. Painted game birds.
Exhib. V.E. (1).

TAYLOR, GEORGE.
Exhib. S.W.L.A. (Sparrowhawk, Thrush, Starling).

TAYLOR, STEPHEN. op. 1817-1837
Resident London, Oxford and Winchester. Painter of animals, portraits and birds, His bird paintings include 'The Tiger cat pouncing upon an Indian Pheasant' (R.A. 1828), 'Mandarin, a Chinese Drake' painted at the London Zoo in 1832.
Exhib. R.A. (48); B.I. (29); S.S. (42).

TAYLOR, W. Op. 1859
Hitchin address.
Exhib. R.A. (1), Game.

TENNENT, JOHN RICHARD MONCRIEFF. b. Singapore 5th November 1926
Member Society of Wildlife Painters. Specialising in birds and landscapes, in particular African subjects. Trained at St. Martin's College of Art. Paints in water-colours, also silk screen prints.
Exhib. S.W.L.A., R.B.A., Clarges Gallery, Oxford Gallery, Bladon Gallery, etc.

THELWELL, DAVID ALAN. b. Birkenhead, 31st March 1950
Water-colour painter of birds. Trained at Norwich School of Art and Southampton College of Art. Resident in Hampshire. His work has been reproduced.
Exhib. S.W.L.A., Pendulum Gallery, Selborne.

THOMAS, Miss D. H. op. 1878-1892
Llandudno address.
Exhib. N.W. (1); V.E. (1), Game.

THOMPSON, RALPH. (living)
Born in Yorkshire, studied at Leeds College of Art and at the Royal College of Art, South Kensington. Illustrated *The Bafut Beagles* published 1954, also *A Brush with Animals* published in 1963. An exhibition of his work shown at the Tryon Gallery, London. Known mainly for his animals but does include bird paintings.

*THORBURN, ARCHIBALD. b. Lasswade, near Edinburgh 31st May 1860, d. 1935
Initially trained by his father, Robert Thorburn, A.R.A., came south to London and was influenced by Joseph Wolf, R.I. He became a well-known writer and illustrator of standard works on British birds and mammals and his reputation was established when he was comissioned to paint a large number of illustrations for Lord Lilford for the latter's *Coloured figures of the Birds of the British Isles* at the end of the 19th century. Later Thorburn published his own works including *British Birds,* 1915-1918, *A Naturalist's Sketch Book* 1919, and *Game Birds and Wildfowl of Great Britain and Ireland,* 1923. He also illustrated numerous other standard works. He painted principally in water-colours although in his earlier days he executed a number of outstanding oil paintings.
Exhib. R.A. (16); S.S. (1); Tryon Gallery, London; Macdonald Booth Gallery, London.
Coll. Belfast, Blackburn, Edinburgh and Preston A.G's.
Repr. *British Sporting Painters.*

*TINNE, DOROTHEA, Mrs. b. Hawkhurst, Kent 1st June 1900
Resident Farnham, Surrey. Mainly painter of animal subjects but does embrace birds in her painting. Studied St John's Wood Art School under Frederick Whalen, and Amsterdam under Herbert van der Poll.
Exhib. R.I., R.B.A., S.W.L.A., Ackerman's Gallery, etc.
Repr. *Love of Lakeland, Signposts to the Wild* and several children's books.

*TODD, CHARLES STANLEY. b. Monkseaton, Northumberland 10th August 1923
Living and working in Perthshire and although self-taught is one of the leading living gamebird and wildlife artists. Has the rare gift of being able to capture the mood and atmosphere of both bird and beast in its natural habitat. Resigned his job in 1956 to study his subjects in the wilder parts of Scotland. Also became an accomplished taxidermist to know his subjects even more closely. The landscape settings for his wild birds are superbly put in.
Exhib. Aberdeen A.G. 1973, John Moncrieff Macmillan Gallery, Perth, 1972, Scottish Game Fair 1973.

Repr. A series of artist-signed proofs from his Wildlife paintings have recently been offered for sale by the John Moncrieff Macmillan Galleries, Perth and London.

*TRELEAVEN, RICHARD BARRIE. b. London 6th July 1920
Living in Cornwall. Studied under the late George E. Lodge. In 1948 started painting sea birds and wildfowl in oils, but now specialises mainly in painting British birds of prey and falconry scenes. Founder member of Society of Wildlife Artists (1963), member British Ornithologists Union (1951), elected to British Falconers Club 1952. First one-man show, Bude (1953) also Launceston (1973). Kept Goshawks, Merlins and Sparrow Hawks, which were trained for falconry and used as live models.
Lit. Author of *The Peregrin in North Cornwall* (Witherby).
Exhib. S.W.L.A., London; Moorland Gallery, London; Art Exhibitions Bureau.

*TUNNICLIFFE, CHARLES FREDERICK, R.A., R.E., A.R.C.A.
b. Langley, East Cheshire 1st December 1901
Painter in water colours, oils, etc. Wood engraver and draughtsman. Trained at Macclesfield School of Art, Manchester School of Art and Royal College of Art. Regular exhibitor at R.A., R.E., Manchester Academy of Art and many provincial galleries.
Coll. R.A., B.M., Belfast A.G., Preston A.G., Johannesburg and many private collections in Britain, America and on the Continent.
Exhib. R.A., S.W.L.A., R.E., etc.
Repr. In many books on wildlife, including *Bird Portraiture* 1945.

TURNER, W.A. fl. 1844
London address.
Exhib. R.A. (1), Wildfowl 1844.

TURTON, W. op. 1830
Whitechurch address.
Exhib. R.A. (1), Game.

TUTHILL, Captain J. V. op. 1847
He sent paintings of birds, 1 to each of the R.A., B.I. and R.S.B.A., in this year.

WALDUCK, D. E. (living)
Exhib. S.W.L.A., Peacocks.

WALES-SMITH, Mrs. ANNE MARY DOROTHY, F.R.H.S. b. Ealing, London 26th December 1934
Bird and animal painter. Member Reading Guild of Artists, Wokingham and district Arts Group. Trained at Thanet School of Art and Ealing Art School. Sometime resident in Bahrein and Singapore. Works in watercolour and gouache.
Exhib. S.W.L.A.; S.W.A.; Century Gallery, Henley; Southern Arts Association (Open Field).

WALKER, G. D. K. op. 1838
Exhib. R.A. (2), Birds.

WARD, VERNON DE BEAUVOIR. b. Hampstead 12th October 1905
Son of Albert Ward, artist, picture expert and antiquarian. Vernon Ward learned to copy all schools of painting in his father's studio under George Fox. At age of 14½ entered the Slade School under Professor Henry Tonks, Sir Walter Russell and Wilson Steer. His great interest in nature resulted from a sketching tour on the Norfolk Broads and birds in particular. Painter of landscape, figure subjects, birds and flowers. Prints of his works have won for him some fame and popularity. One of his paintings 'Wildfowl leaving Arran' S & D 1946 was sold at Christie's 22nd January 1965. Other paintings include 'Dawn – Mallard coming in'; 'Flight over Sky'; 'Shovellers frightened'; 'Spring Ecstasy' (Ducks); 'Wild Alarm' (Mallard), etc.

*WARREN, MICHAEL JOHN. b. Wolverhampton 26th October 1938
Member of the Society of Wildlife Astists. Trained at Wolverhampton College of Art. Spent 9 years in Interior Design prior to painting birds full time, a probable influence of his use of colour. His subjects derived

from field observation and his style original and decorative with detailed emphasis on the bird. Uses skins as reference and Chinese ink as his medium.
Exhib. S.W.L.A.; Moorland Gallery, London (one-man show); Tryon Galleries, London and Nairobi.

WATERFIELD, KENNETH JOHN. b. Watford, Herts. 7th November 1927
Resident in Hampshire. His wildlife paintings are an extension and development of his landscape work. Paints in oil, acrylic and water-colour in varying degrees of abstraction. The coloured cover made for *Birds* (July/August 1973) being a typical example of his particular style. Trained Watford School of Art.
Repr. *Birds* the R.S.P.B. Magazine (July/August 1973).
Exhib. S.W.L.A.; Tryon Gallery, London; Southampton City A.G.; Ashbarn Gallery, Petersfield, etc.

WATERS, BILLIE. b. Richmond 1896
Flower and animal painter (including birds).
Exhib. R.A., N. G. and Society of Wood Engravers.
Repr. 'Crested Grebe & water lilies' (Homelovers prints) Frost & Reed Ltd., *Sphere, Studio.*

*WATSON, DONALD. b. Cranleigh, Surrey 28th June 1918.
Living in Galloway, S.W. Scotland since 1951, the region having been subjects for many paintings, drawings and writings. President, Scottish Ornithologists' Club (1969-1972). Founder member of Society of Wildlife Artists. Has held one-man exhibitions. Painter in water-colour, gouache, oils, black and white scraper board. No Art College training, but B.A. (Hons) Oxon. with specialised interest in renaissance art. Married Joan Dudley Moore (1950), four children.
Exhib. Royal Scottish Academy; Royal Scottish Society of Painters in Water-colour; One-man exhibitions, London, Edinburgh, Glasgow, Newcastle, Oxford, Bristol, Dumfries, and also exhibits in various groups, etc.
Coll. Glasgow A.G.; Ulster Museum & A.G.; Gracefield A.G., Dumfries.
Repr. Illustrator and author of ornithological Books *Birds of Moor & Mountain* (1972). *Birdwatchers' Year* (1973). *Oxford Book of Birds* (1964), etc. Contributor of drawings and articles to various journals.

*WATSON, RAYMOND CYRIL. b. Codenham Green, Suffolk 25th March 1935
Member Armed Forces Art Society and Ipswich Art Club. Trained at Ipswich Art. School. Paints in water-colour.
Exhib. The Moorland Gallery since the mid 1960's. Has had several successful one-man exhibitions. The Tryon Gallery (Bird Artists of the World) 1972. Budapest (The World Hunting Exhibition) 1971. His picture 'Red-breasted Geese' won the award for Great Britain in the Fine Art Section.
Coll. Ulster Museum and many private collections in America and Europe.

WEATHERBY, J. op. 1823-1824
A resident at Newmarket, where, as an amateur, he painted birds. He showed 2 works at the R.A., 1 at the B.I.

WEATHERLY, RICHARD. b. 1947
An Australian reared on his family's sheep station in Victoria where at an early age he taught himself to carve in wood the animals of the surrounding outback. His paintings were a natural outcome from his working sketches. He came to this country a few years ago and studied under some of our leading bird artists; he has since painted birds in Africa, Australia and Britain.
Exhib. Sladmore Gallery 1970 in 'The World's Wildlife' exhibition, and in 1972 combining with Bryan Reed in a two-man show at the same Gallery. Also shows work at the S.W.L.A.

WEEKES, WILLIAM. op. 1864-1904
Not exactly a bird painter, but his works, often humourous, did comprise birds and very well painted too. His subjects were mainly domestic, and farmyard animals in humourous situations were his speciality. He had a passion for Donkeys in this vein, of which 'The Connoisseurs', five donkeys standing and viewing a painting on an easel, is a nexample. Others were titled 'Prattlers & Cacklers', 'The Patient and the Quacks', etc. Of the family of Henry Weekes, R.A.
Exhib. R.A. (49); B.I. (11); S.S. (10).
Repr. *Country Life,* 28th February 1974 (advert). A pair of paintings of Hens (Oscar & Peter Johnson Ltd.)

WEIR, HARRISON WILLIAM. b. Lewes 5th May 1824, d. Appledore, Kent 3rd January 1906
Educated at Camberwell. Learnt the art of colour printing under George Baxter, leaving to become an independant artist. He built himself a great reputation for his studies of birds and animals. Contributed drawings to the *Illustrated London News,* the *Graphic, Black and White,* and other periodicals, and his illustrations appeared in many books. Author of *Poultry and all about them.* Elected Associate of the N.W.C.S., now the R.I., in 1849, a member in 1851, but retired in 1870. Friend of Darwin, a keen naturalist, a lover of animals and a champion of their cause. His first wife was the eldest daughter of J. F. Herring (1795-1865) the well-known sporting painter.
Exhib. R.A. (6); B.I. (3); S.S. (4).
Coll. V. & A. Department of E.I.D. have several of his sketch books containing birds and animals.

WELLS, L. JENNENS. op. 1865-1868
Exhib. V.E. (3), Birds.

WHALLEY, PATRICK D.
Exhib. The Sladmore Gallery, London 1973.

WHITEFORD, SIDNEY TREFUSIS. op. 1860-1881
Plymouth and London addresses. Painter of genre, still life, birds and flowers.
Exhib. R.A. (1869-1881). His 1880 exhibit was titled *British Birds.*

WHYMPER, CHARLES, R.I. b. 1853, d. 1941
A large proportion of his output is contained in black and white illustrations in late 19th century books on birds, big game and other animals. He provided the 40 or more colour illustrations for Dixon's *Game Birds & Wildfowl of the British Islands* published in a revised edition in 1900. His work can vary from the 'tightness' required in book illustrations to a very attractive 'loose' water-colour approach. He also painted some fine oils in the manner of his master, Joseph Wolf, R.I.
Exhib. The Macdonald Booth Gallery, London.
N.B. *The Connoisseur,* commenting on his bird subjects at the R.I. in 1922, says: 'His work relies on an almost scientific presentment correct to the last detail of the feathered creatures which he chooses to depict.'

WICKSTEAD, J. (or Wicksteed)
Probably related to C. F. Wicksteed (op. 1790-1846), the son of James Wicksteed (or Wickstead), an engraver (b. 1719, d. London 11th July 1791), all the family being thus alternately spelt. There is also Philips Wickstead, the portrait-painting pupil of Zoffany. Frost & Reed exhibited a 'Portrait of a Fighting Cock, trimmed and spurred' recently. Given as J. Wickstead.

WILLIAMS, J. M. op. 1834-1849
London address. Painted Landscapes, castles, ruins, birds and sporting subjects. Visited Waterloo and Antwerp. R.A. exhibit in 1840 'Ptarmigan and Wood Pigeons', and 'Wild Ducks' in 1841.
Exhib. R.A. (8); B.I. (8); S.S. (9); N.W.C.S. (1).

*WILLIAMSON-BELL, JAMES. b. Tynemouth 25th September 1938
Bird painter, resident in Newcastle-on-Tyne. Exhibits at numerous galleries in the United Kingdom. Painting mostly in water-colour, gouache, acrylic and pen and ink.
Exhib. Royal Society of Miniature Painters, Sculptors & Gravers, 1973. Royal Society of Painter-Etchers & Gravers, 1974. Paris Salon, 1974. Also at Setanta Gallery, Dublin; James Alder Ltd. and S.W.L.A.
Repr. The Medici Society, London.

*WILLIS, IAN ROBERT. b. Hexham, Northumberland, 18th March 1944
Painter of birds and mammals, also book illustrator. Contributor on his subject to various magazines. Has been on expeditions, and shorter trips to much of Europe, including a sojourn of ten months in Turkey. Paints in gouache and recently in water-colour. Trained at Brighton College of Art.
Coll. Ulster Museum, Belfast.
Exhib. Brighton, 1956 (one-man show) sponsored by the Royal Society for the Protection of Birds. Also

various exhibitions organised by the R.S.P.B. and British Trust for Ornithology. S.W.L.A. (annual and travelling exhibitions).
Repr. *Birds of the Western Palearctic* (one of the illustrators). *Flight Shapes and Patterns of European Raptors*', making over 300 drawings. *Predatory Birds in Britain* (Council for Nature). Cover design (Snow Buntings) for *Birds,* (March/April issue) for R.S.P.B.

WILSHER, JON DAVID.
Exhib. S.W.L.A. (Eagle Owl).

WILSHER, T. op. 1816
Exhib R.A. (1), Birds. Possibly same as T. Wilshire.

WILSHIRE, T. op. 1816
He sent a painting of 'A Bird' to the R.A. in this year.

WILSON, MAURICE CHARLES JOHN, R.I. b. London 1st March 1914
Member of R.I. and S.W.L.A. Painter of birds and animal life, etc. Trained at Hastings School of Art and Royal Academy Schools. Taught at Bromley School of Art and at Royal School of Needlework (plant drawing, etc.). Has illustrated a number of books, a number of greeting cards and prints reproduced from his works. Resident at Bidborough, Kent.
Exhib. R.A., R.S.M.A., R.I., S.W.L.A., some commercial Galleries and travelling exhibitions.
Coll. Natural History Museum.

WINDER, J.T. op. 1875
Exhib. R.A. (1), Birds.

WINGFIELD, J. op. 1791-1798
Painter of animals, birds, fish and flowers in landscape settings. Exhibited 8 examples at the R.A.
Exhib. R.A. (8), including 'Larks' 1791, 'Wild Duck and Widgeon' 1792, 'Pheasants' 1793, 'Wild Fowl' 1796.

WITHERINGTON, WILLIAM FREDERICK, R.A.
b. London 25th May 1785, d. London 10th April 1865
Exhibited 'Partridges' at the R.A. in 1812, but not generally a bird painter.

WITHERS, Mrs. AUGUSTUS INNES, R.B.A. op. 1829-1865
Painter of flowers, fruit and birds. Appointed Flower Painter in Ordinary to the Queen Dowager in 1833. Member of the Society of Lady Artists.
Exhib. R.A., S.S., N.W.C.S. and V.E.

WOLF, JOSEPH, R.I. b. Morz, nr. Coblenz 21st January 1820, d. London 20th April 1899
Painter of animals and birds. From early youth fond of birds, watching and drawing them. Apprenticed for 3 years to the brothers Becker, lithographers of Coblenz, later becoming a lithographer at Darmstadt. Then to Antwerp where he painted bird pictures. Then to London in 1848 obtaining employment at the British Museum. Drew for a large number of books on natural history, including John Gould's *Birds of Great Britain* and *Birds of Asia.* Made drawings for the Zoological Society also.
Exhib. From 1841-1881 at R.A., B.I., R.I.
Coll. V. & A. have numerous drawings of birds.
Lit. *Life of Joseph Wolf* by A. H. Palmer (1895).

WOOD, KENNETH JAMES. b. Redhill, Surrey 8th May 1936
Self-taught artist, painting mainly in water-colour and from observation made in the field and from detailed anatomical studies of dead specimens. He is a Falconer and has trained Kestrel, Merlin, Sparrow Hawk, Red-headed Falcon and Goshawk. Represented in a number of private collections, educational authorities, etc.
Exhib. S.W.L.A. (annually).
Repr. Medici Society and R.S.P.B.

WOODFORD, Miss ROSEMARY. b. Melbury Osmond, Dorset 18th March 1949
Trained Bournemouth & Poole College of Art, after which self-taught. Specialising in East African wildlife, having lived for three years in the Queen Elizabeth National Park (now known as the Ruwenzori National Park) in Uganda. Uses water-colour and acrylic gouache.
Exhib. S.W.L.A., Tryon Galleries, London and Nairobi, and The Nairobi Galleries.

WOODHOUSE, WILLIAM. b. Poulton-le-Sands 1st October 1857, d. Morecambe 13th January 1939
Woodhouse possessed, at an early age, a love of nature and became a student at the Lancaster School of Art. In 1899 he made an extensive tour of the Near East, visiting Turkey, Greece and the Mediterranean. An independent artist who rarely exhibited outside Lancashire – 1 work only at the R.A. in 1889; a few others at the R.I. and R.S.A. Exhibited at the Walker Art Gallery, Liverpool, and regularly in the Lancashire Art Exhibition at Preston from 1927 until his death. A memorial exhibition of some 89 works, mostly animals, was held at Preston in 1939. His works included birds. The Fine Art Publishing Company, London, made photogravure reproductions of many of his works.
Coll. Harris Museum & A.G., Preston (Snipe) October 1943, no. 130.

WOODROUFFE, R. op. 1825-1854
London address. Painter of game birds and animals, mostly in the Highlands.
Exhib. R.A. (4); B.I. (4).

WOORT, T.W. op. 1873
A 'Partridges on a Hillside' S&D 1873, sold at Sotheby's 28th October 1964.

WRIGHT, HELENA A. op. 1883
Nottingham address.
Exhib. S.S. (1), Game.

WRIGHT, WILLIAM P. op. 1882
Exhib. S.S. (1), Birds.

YOUNG, JEAN, R.B.A., N.E.A.C. b. Hampstead 1914
Trained at The Polytechnic, London; at the London Zoo under John Skeaping, R.A.; five years at the Royal Academy Schools, and at Florence. Works mainly in oils. Illustrator of several books. Paintings have been acquired by many County Councils and private collectors in England and the United States of America.
Exhib. R.A.; Leicester Galleries; R.B.A.; N.E.A.C.; S.W.A.; S.W.L.A.

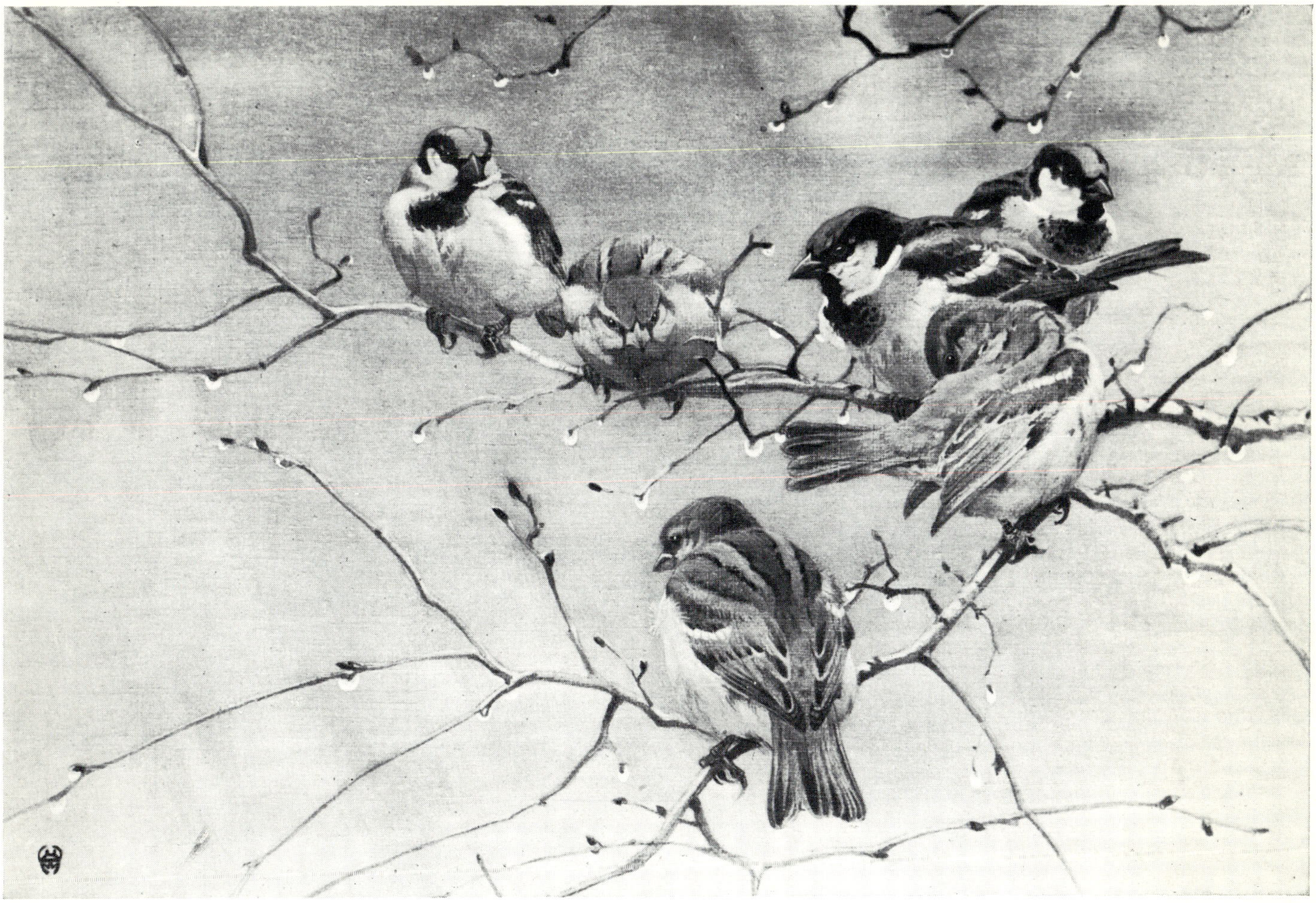

WINIFRED AUSTEN, R.E., R.I.
Rogues & Vagabonds
Courtesy, Harris Museum & Art Gallery, Preston

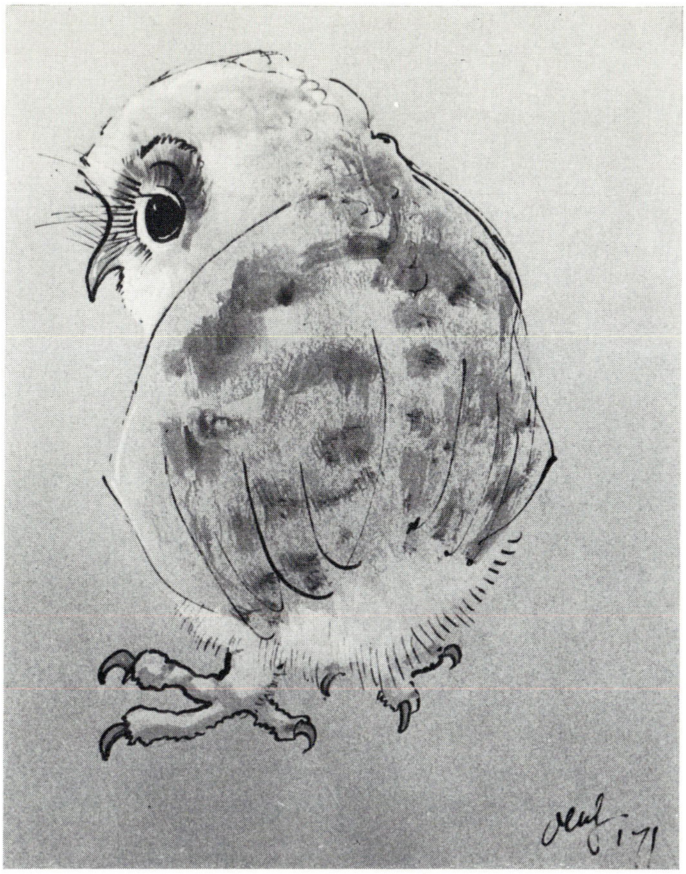

SYLVIA C. BALL
Tawny Owlett

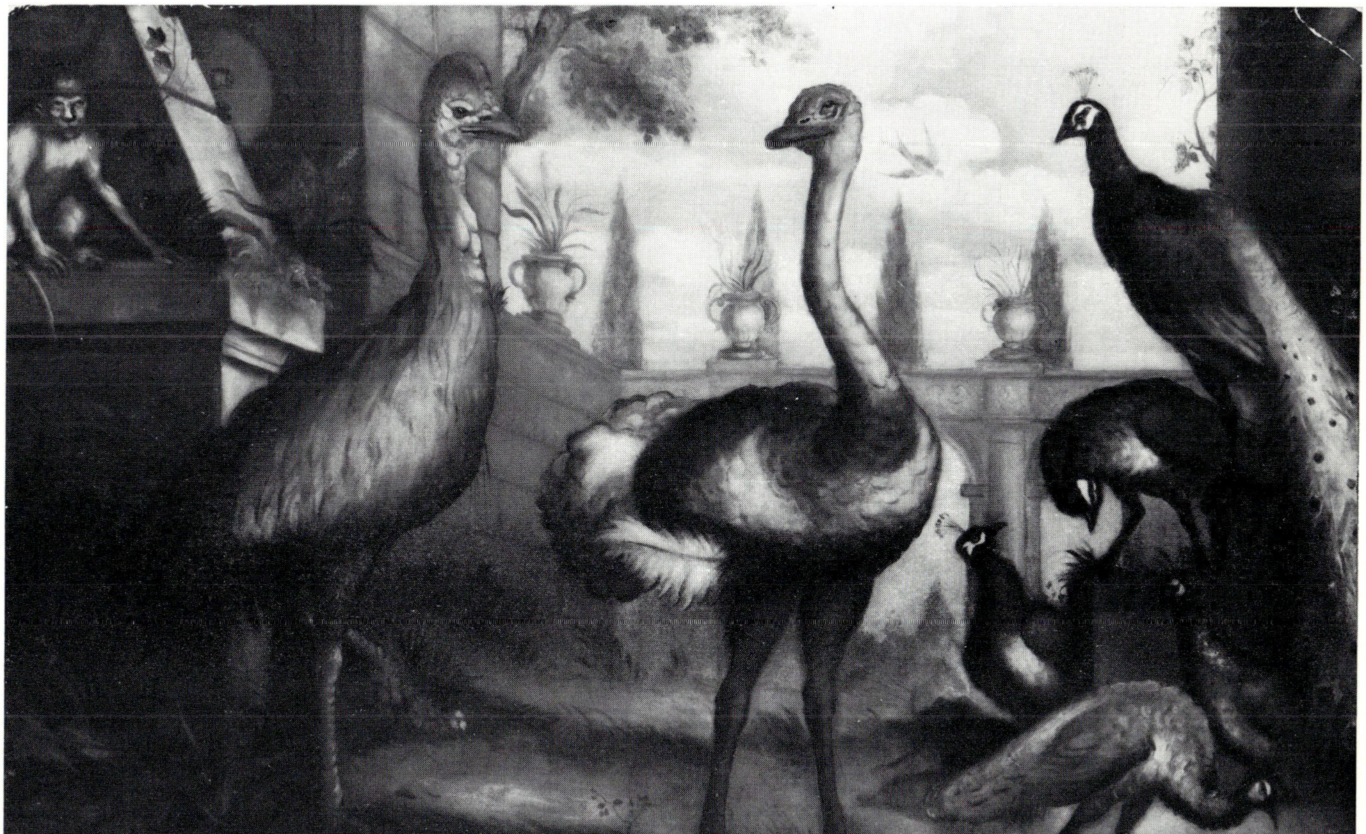

FRANCIS BARLOW
Ostriches, Peacocks & other Birds
Courtesy, Oscar & Peter Johnson Ltd, London

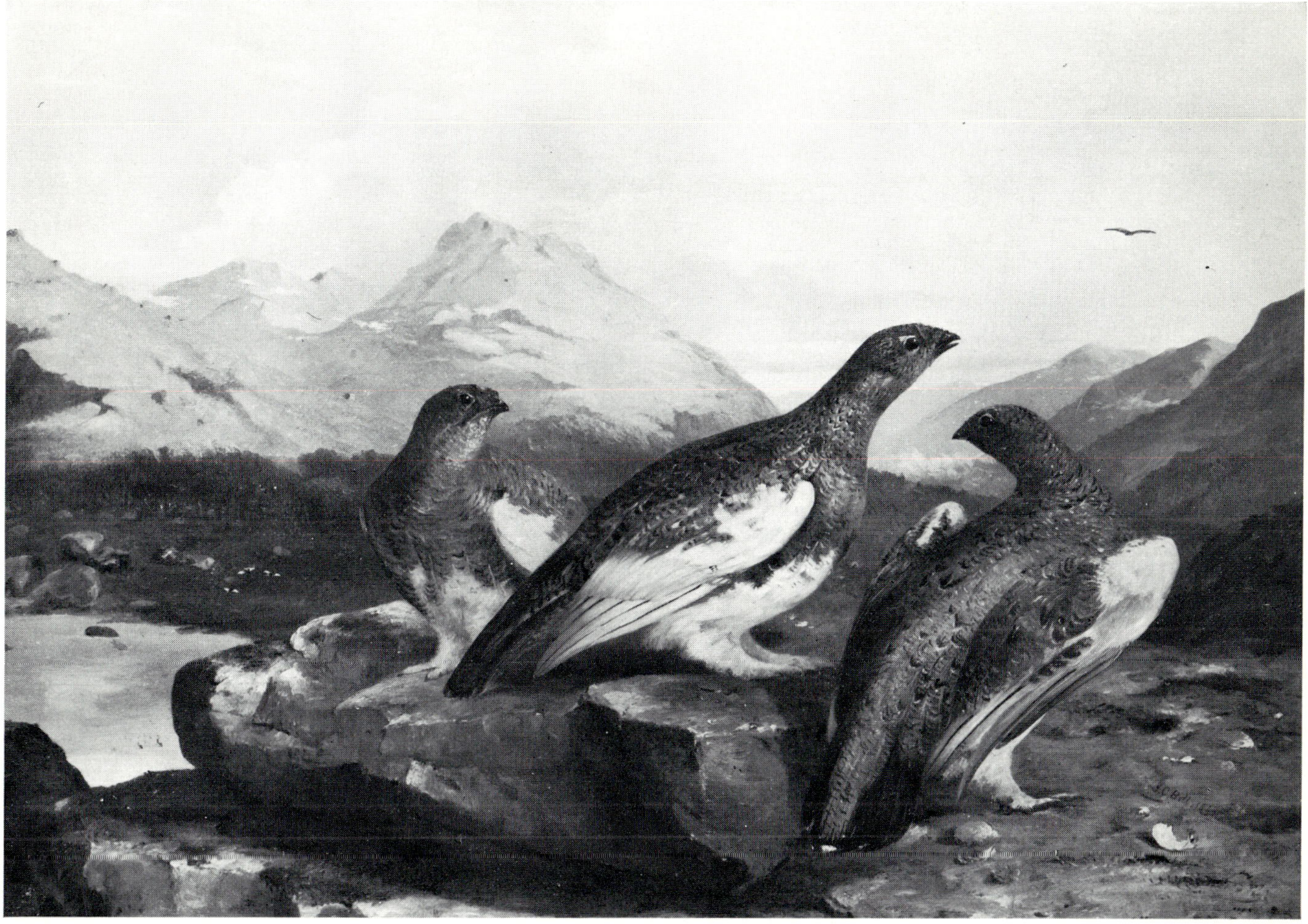

J. C. BELL
Ptarmigan
Courtesy, Mr. & Mrs. Dewitte L. Sage
(Photograph, Spink & Sons Ltd)

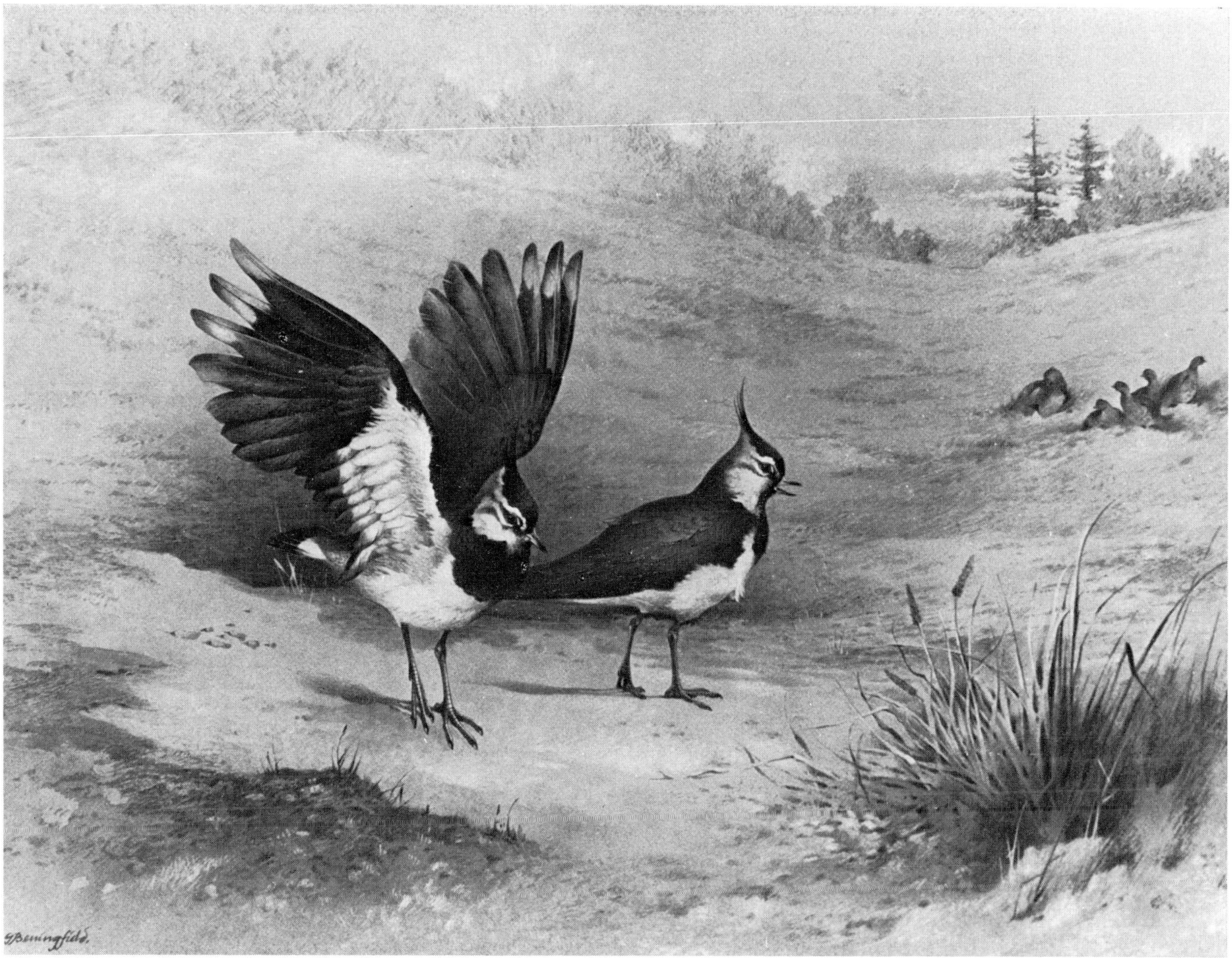

GORDON GEORGE BENINGFIELD
Lapwings

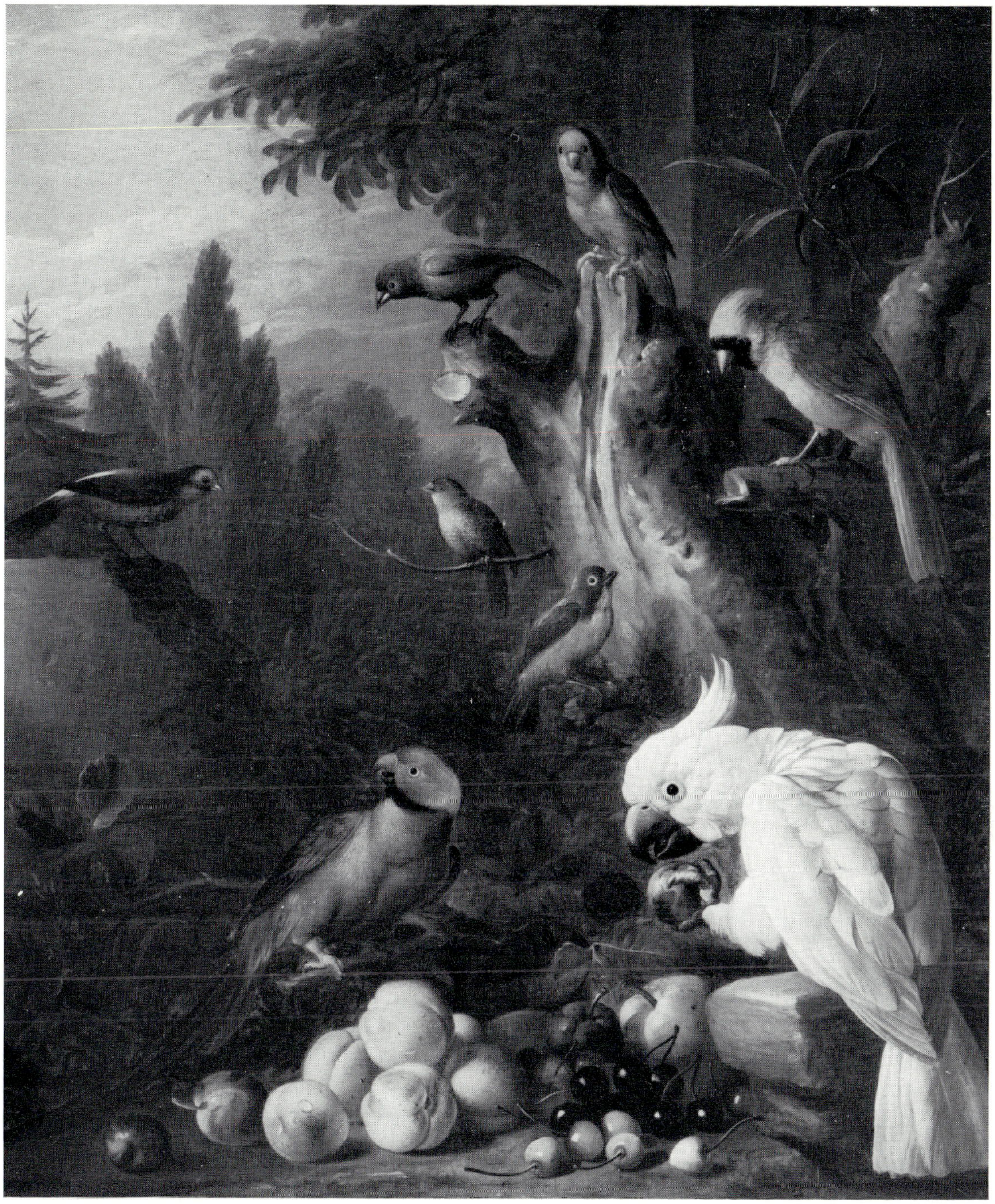

JACOB BOGDANI
Exotic Birds
Courtesy, Sotheby & Co, London

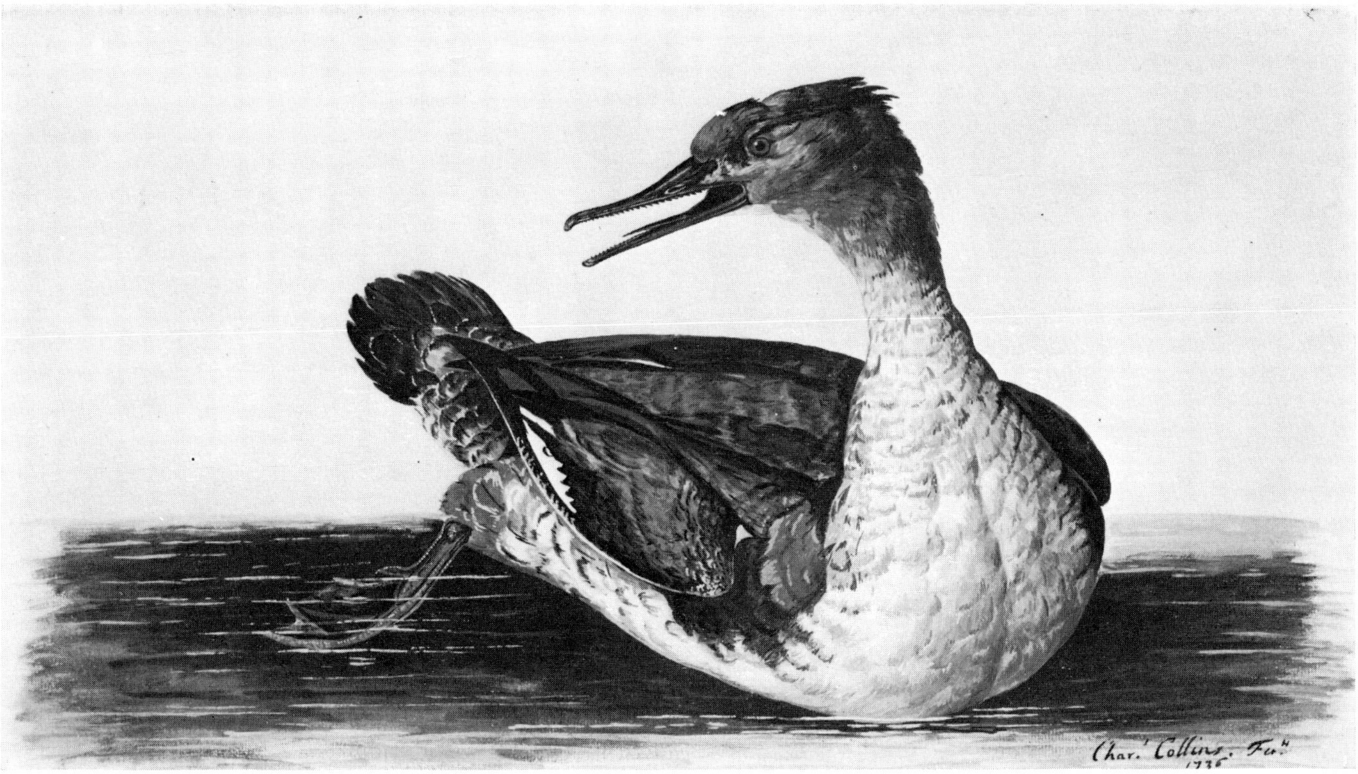

CHARLES COLLINS
Merganser (female)
Courtesy, Spink & Son Ltd, London

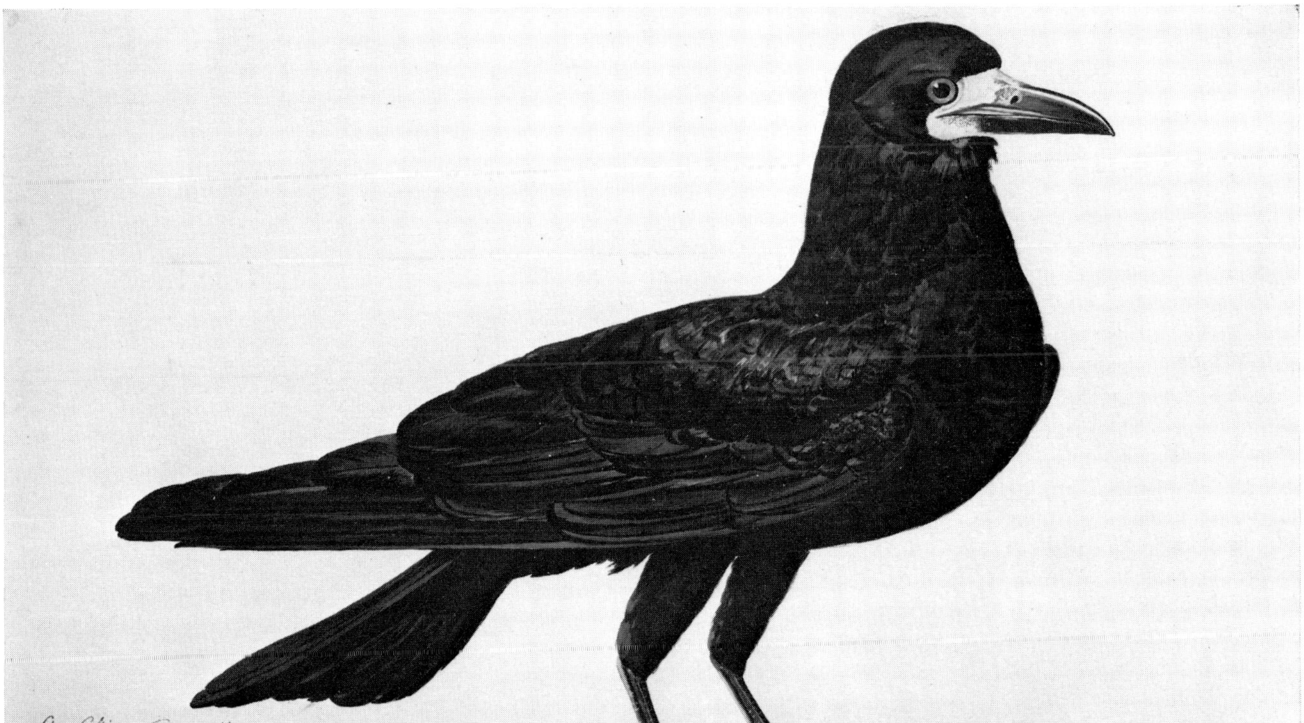

CHARLES COLLINS
Rook
Courtesy, Spink & Son Ltd, London

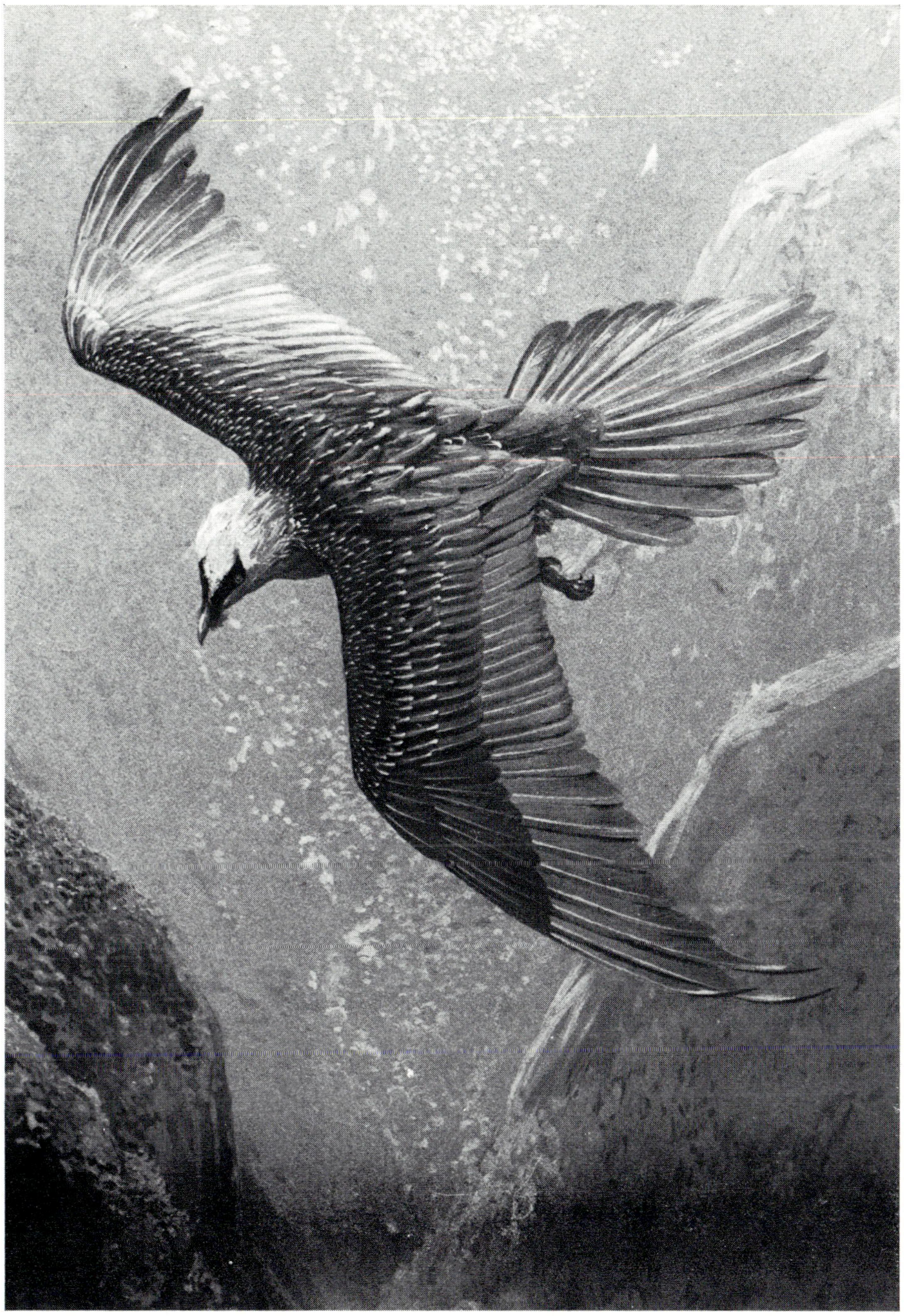

Dr. CHARLES JOHN FRANKLIN COOMBS
Lammereier – Pyrenees

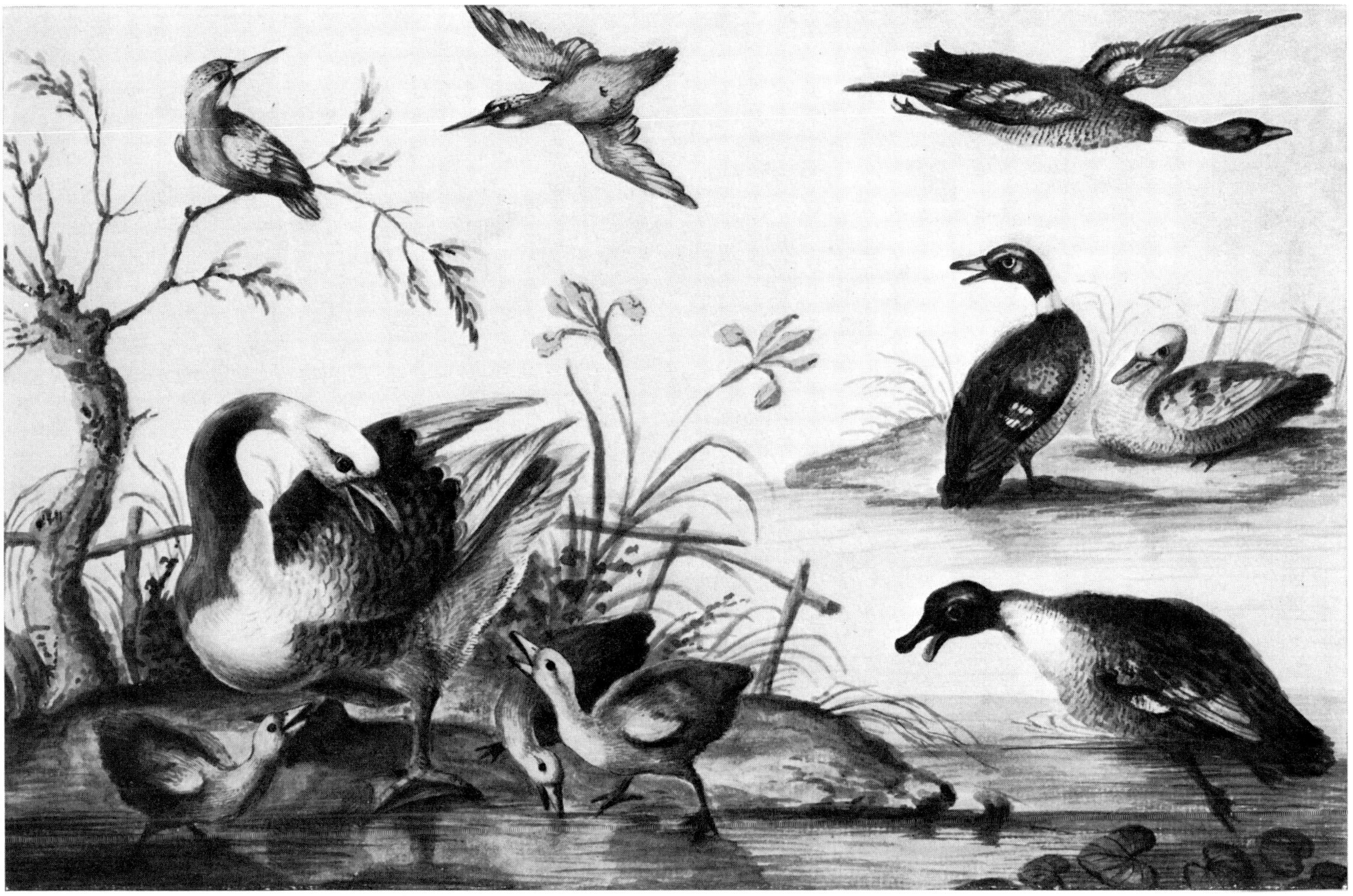

MARMADUKE CRADOCK
Various Birds
Courtesy, The Leger Galleries, London

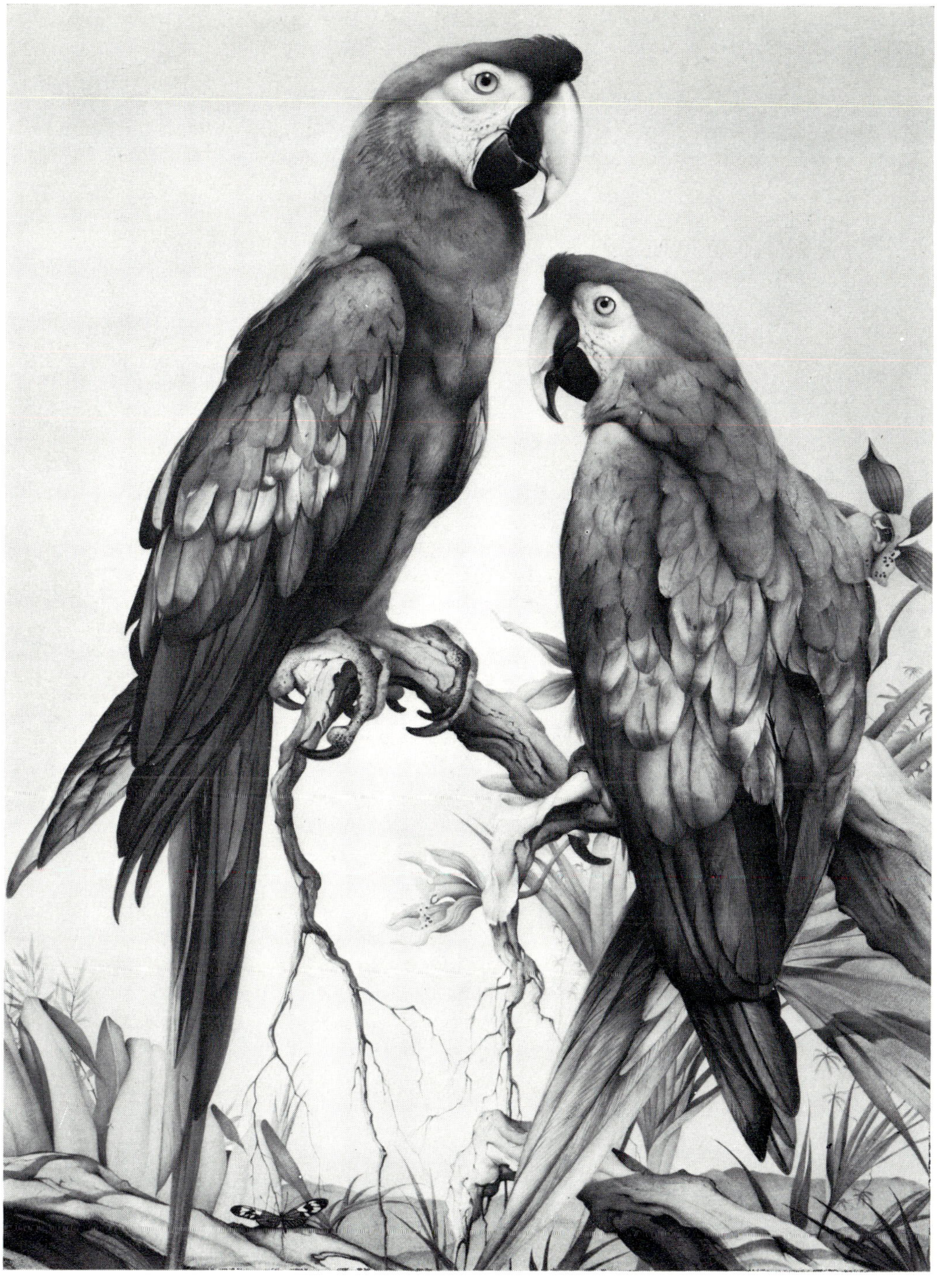

EDWARD JULIUS DETMOLD
Two Macaws with Orchids and a Butterfly
Courtesy, The Leger Galleries, London

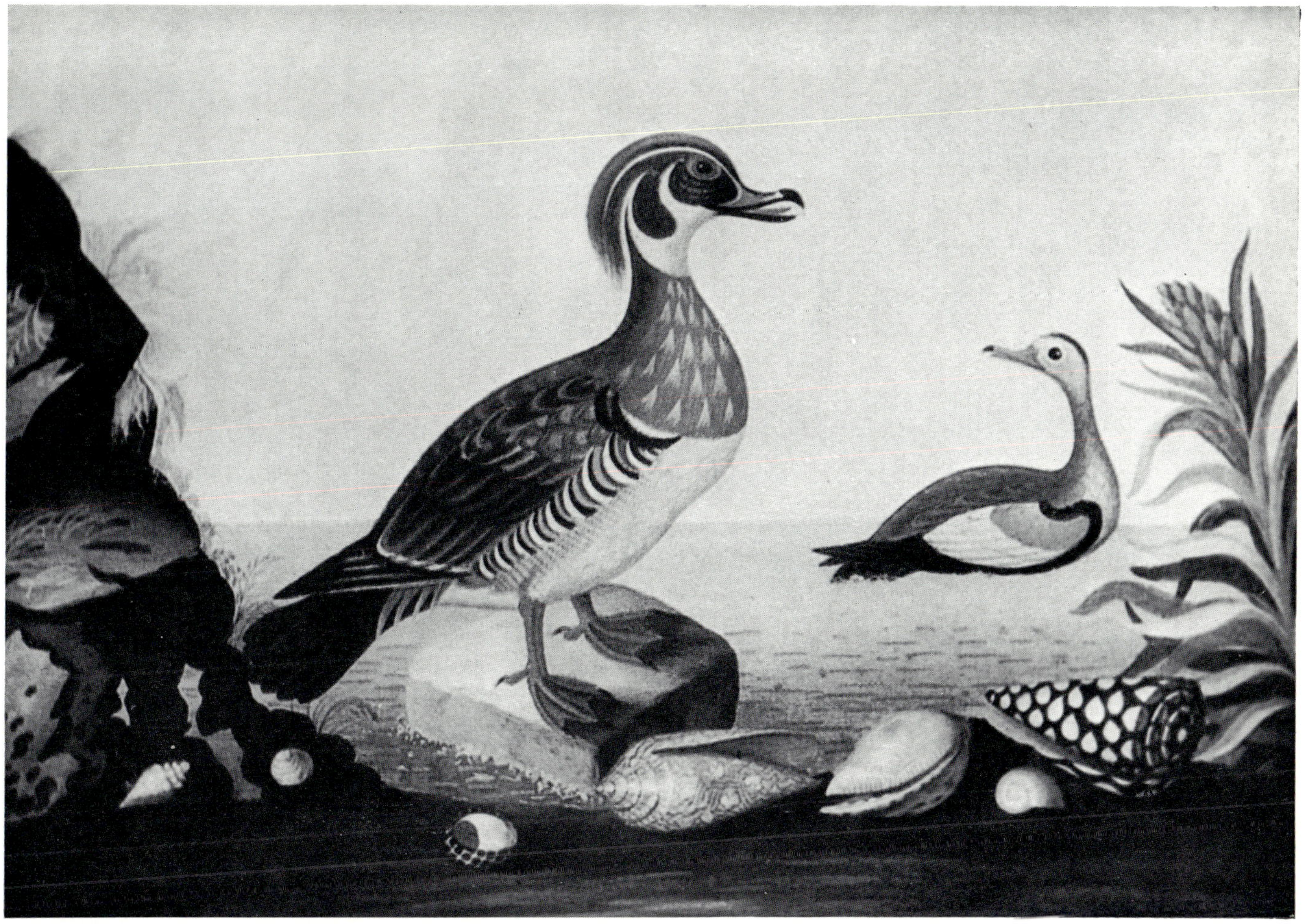

SAMUEL DIXON
Summer & Red-billed Whistling Duck

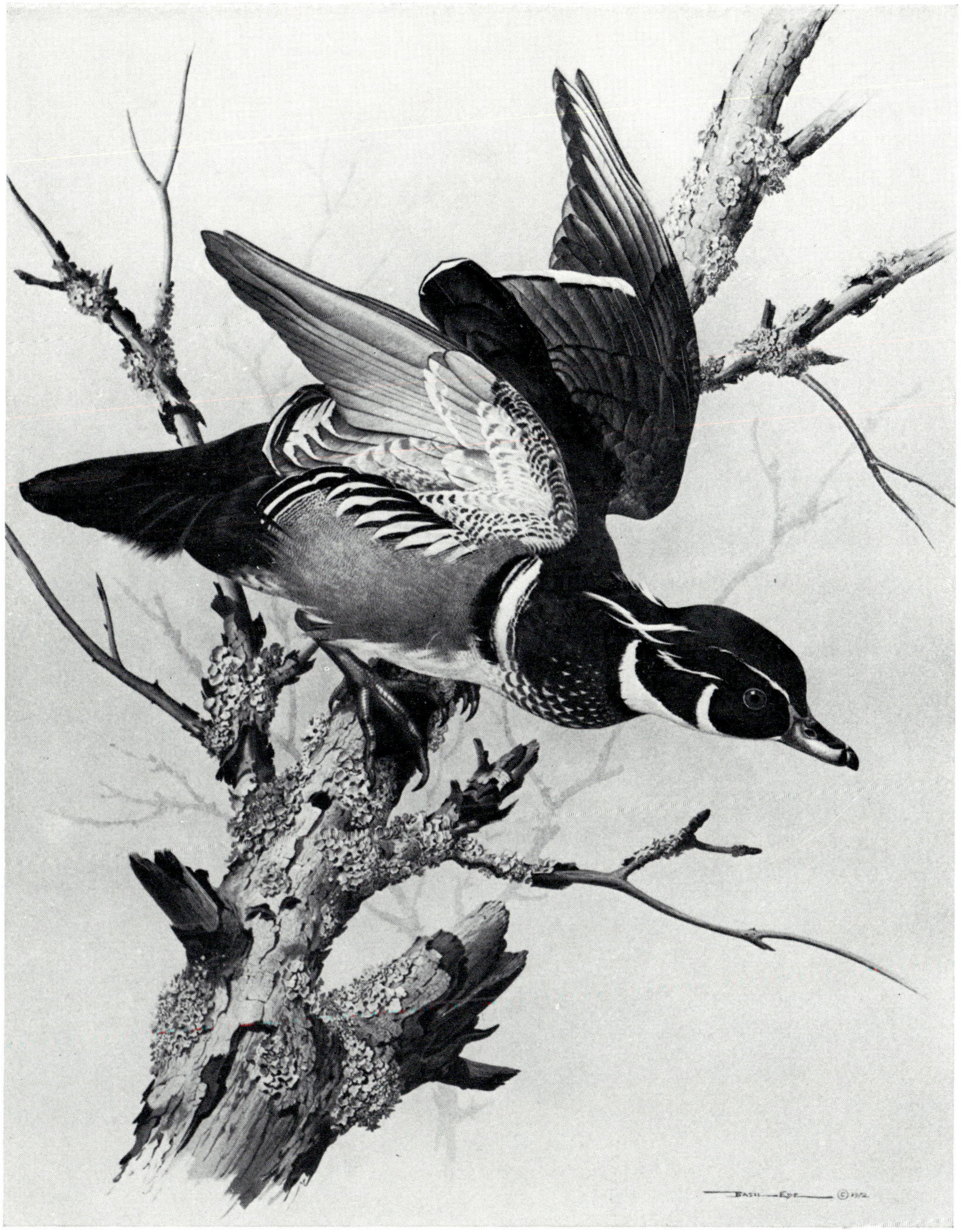

BASIL EDE
Carolina Wood Duck
Courtesy, Gulf States Paper Corporation, Alabama, U.S.A.

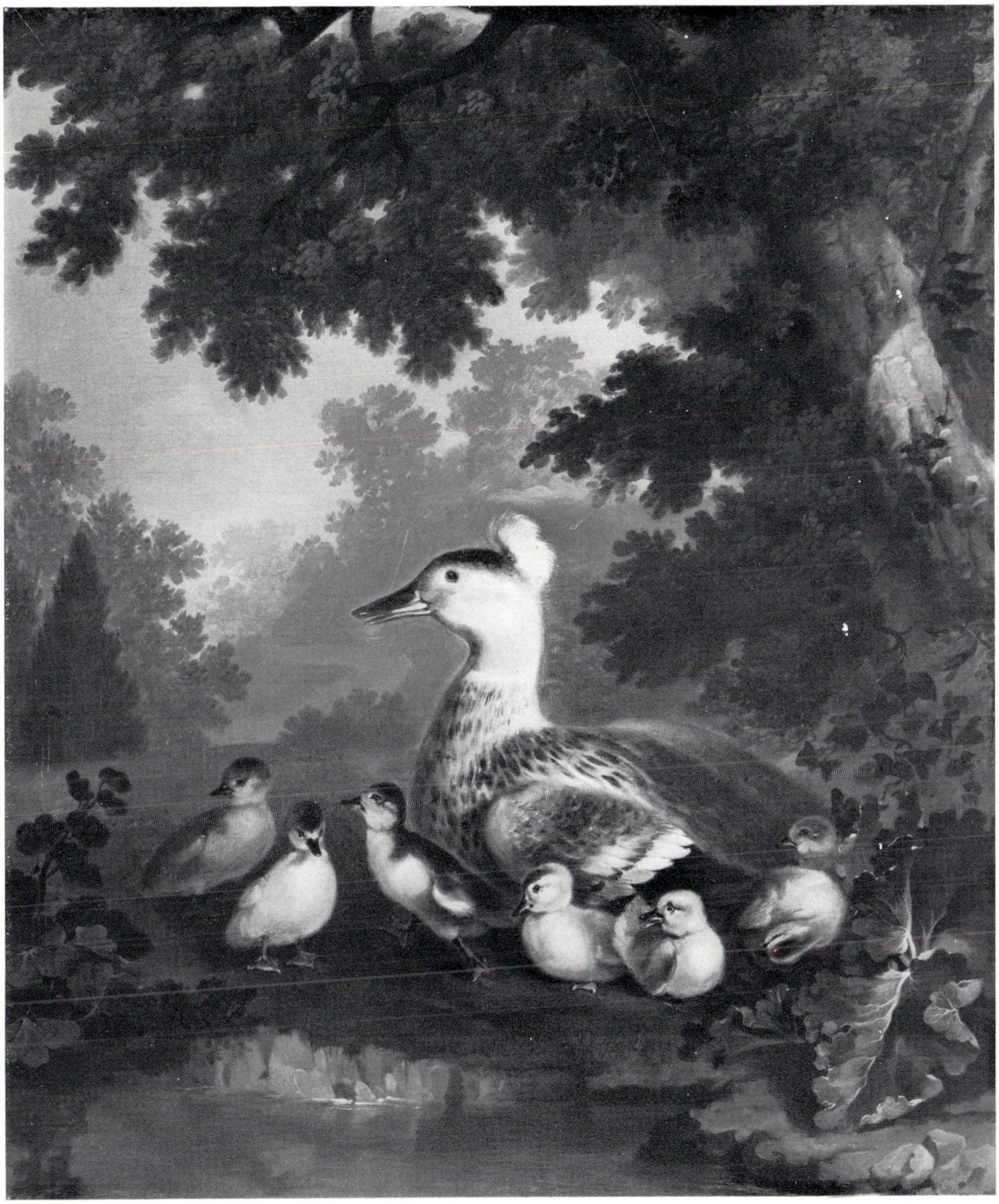

JOHN EDWARDS
Duck and Ducklings (Hooded Merganser)
Courtesy, Spink & Son Ltd, London

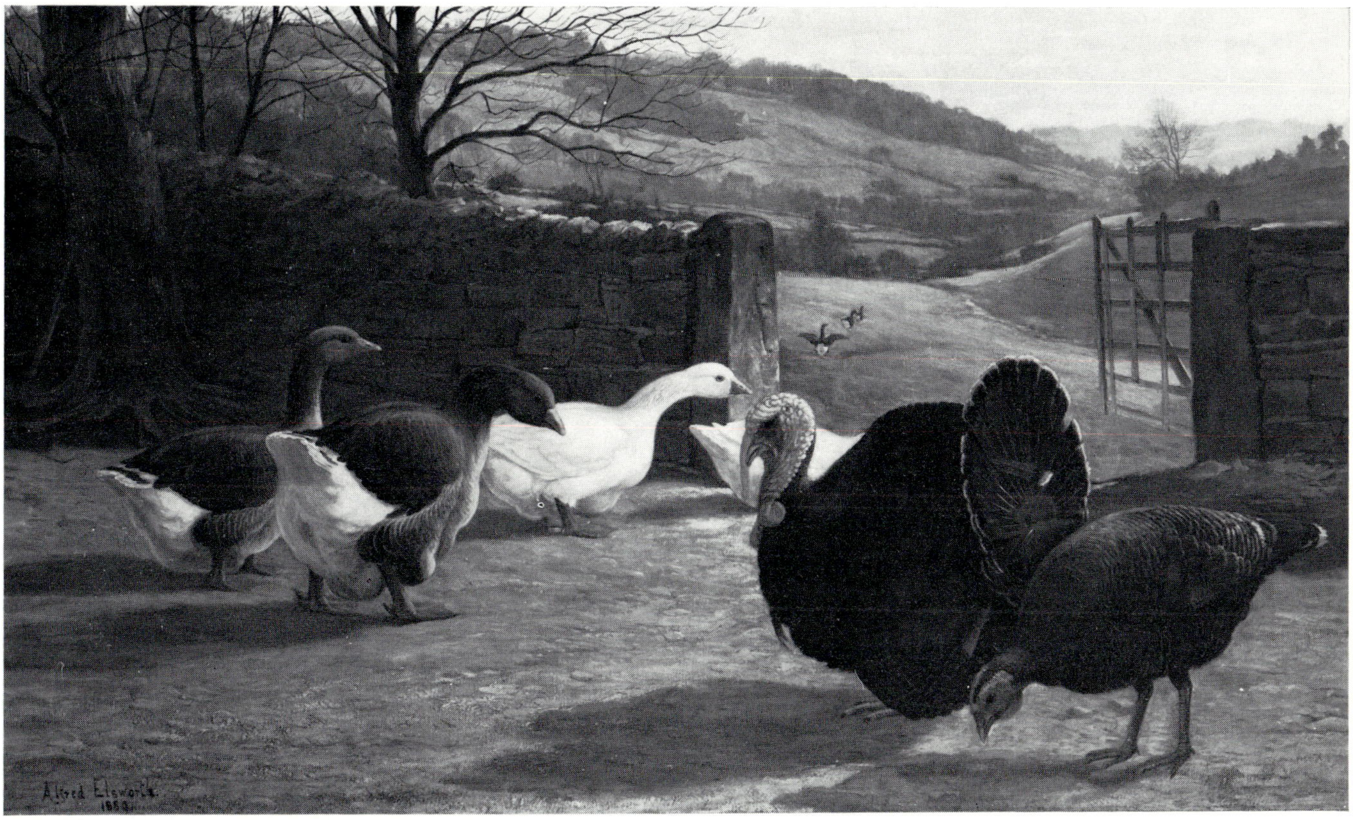

ALFRED ELSWORTH
Farmyard scene with Geese & Turkeys
Courtesy, Oscar & Peter Johnson Ltd, London

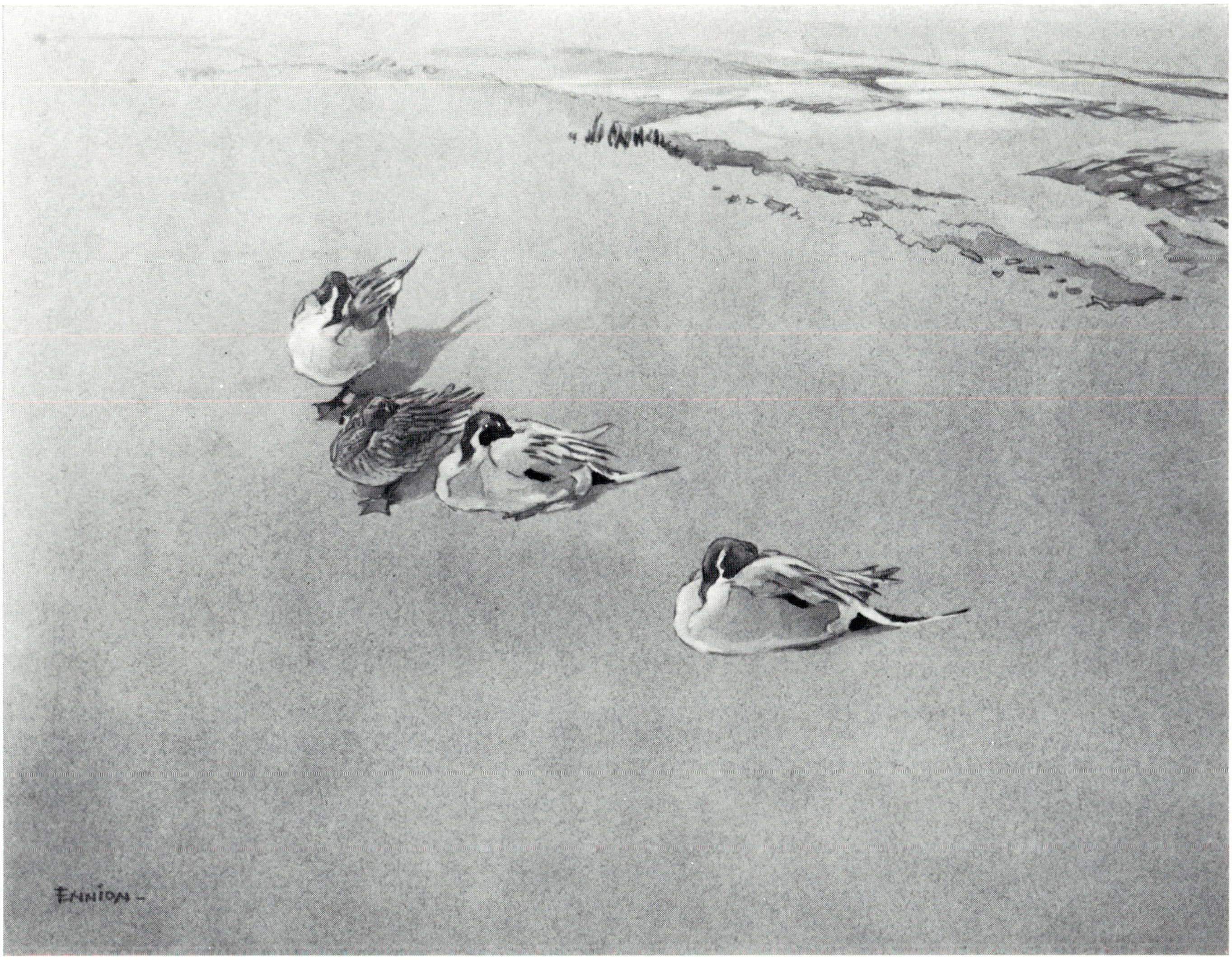

Dr. ERIC ENNION
Pintail Resting

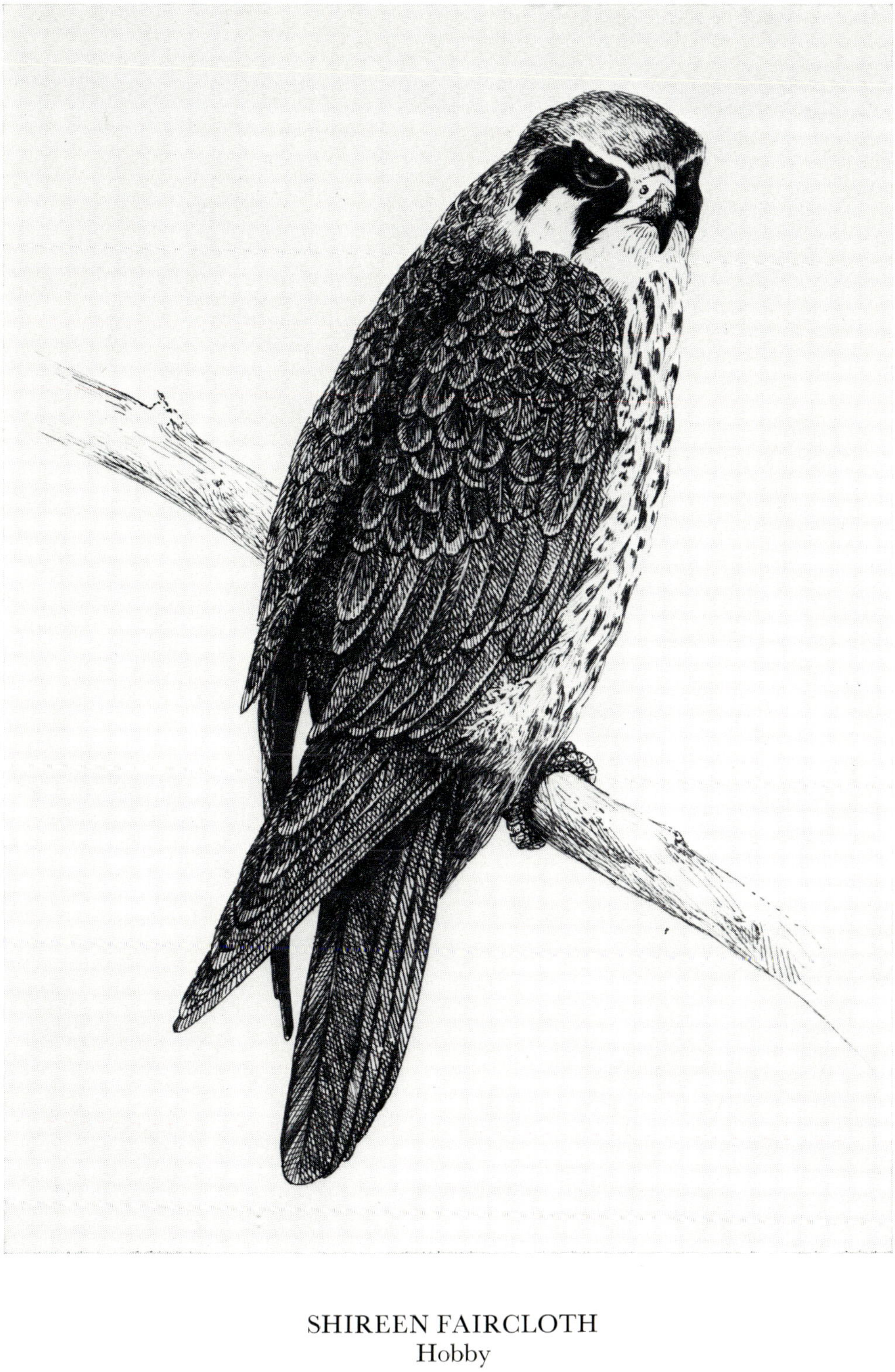

SHIREEN FAIRCLOTH
Hobby

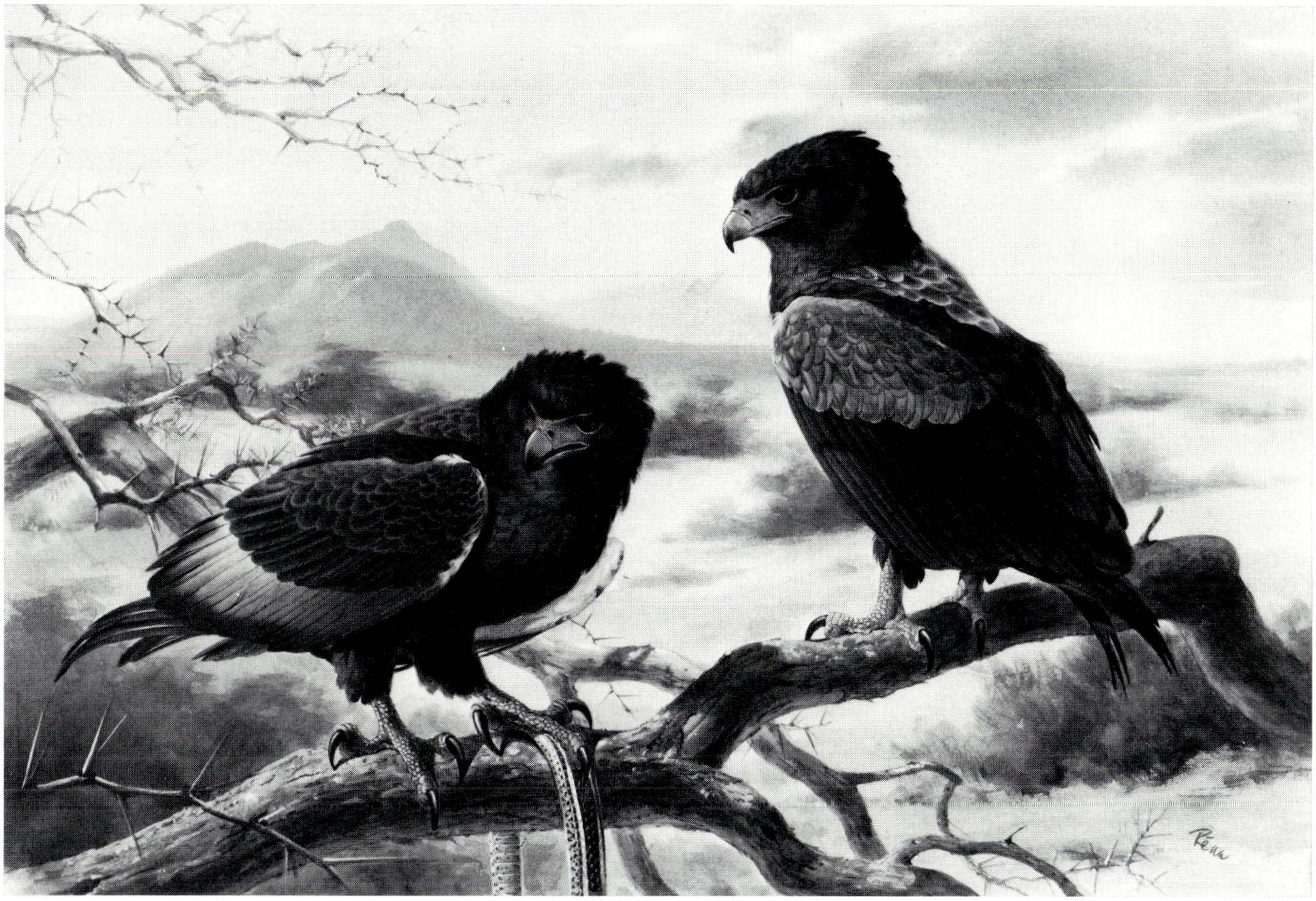

RENA MARGARET FENNESSY
Bateleur Eagles
Courtesy, The Tryon Gallery Ltd, London

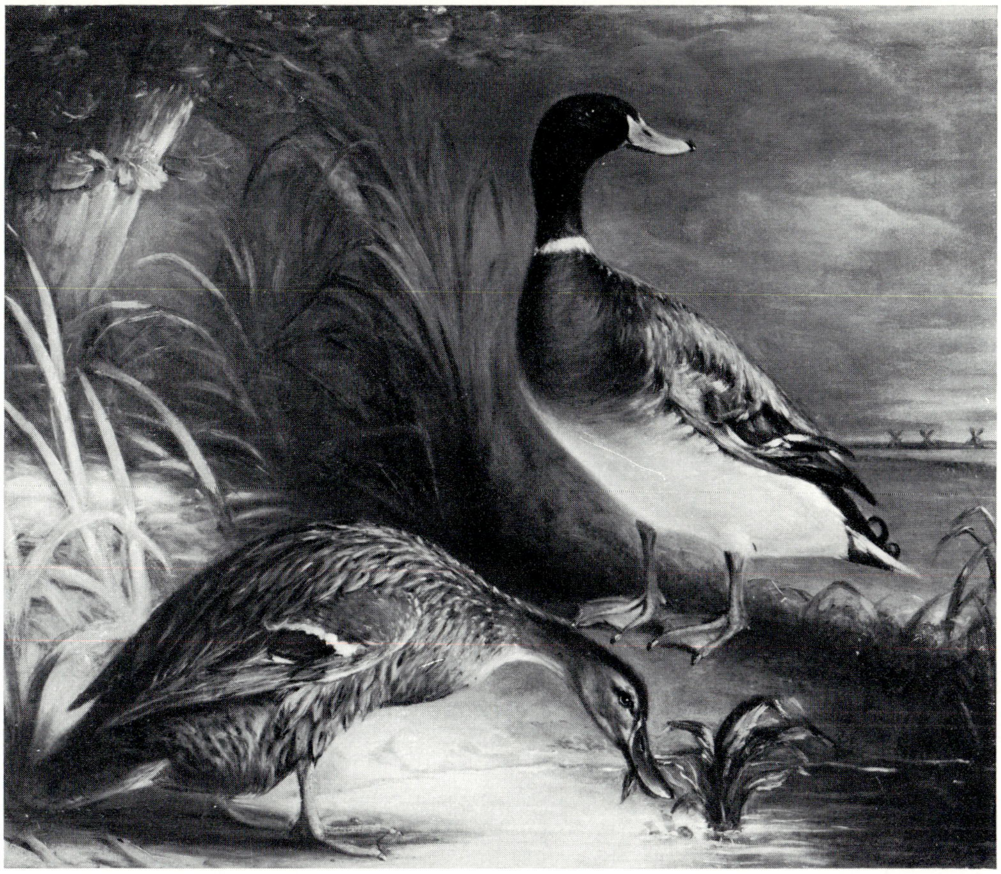

JOHN E. FERNELEY
Duck & Drake
Courtesy, Berry Hill Galleries Inc, New York

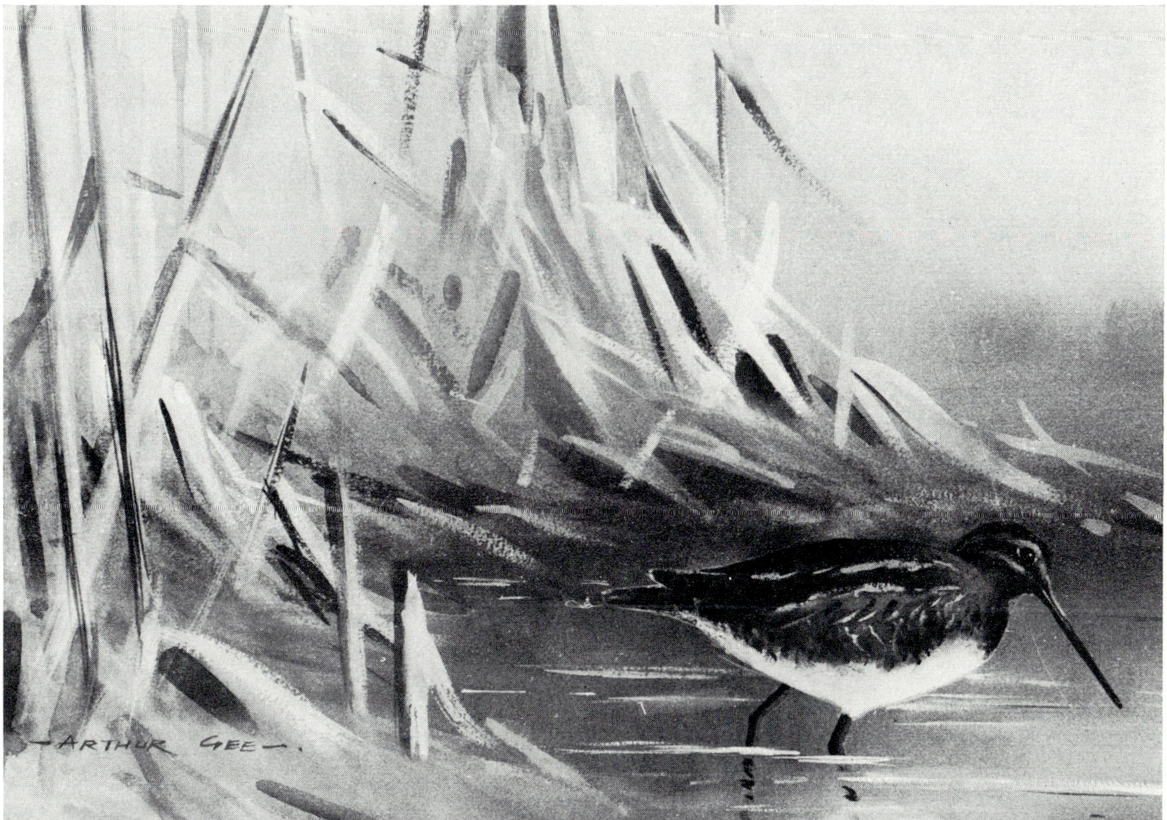

ARTHUR GEE
Snipe in the Reeds

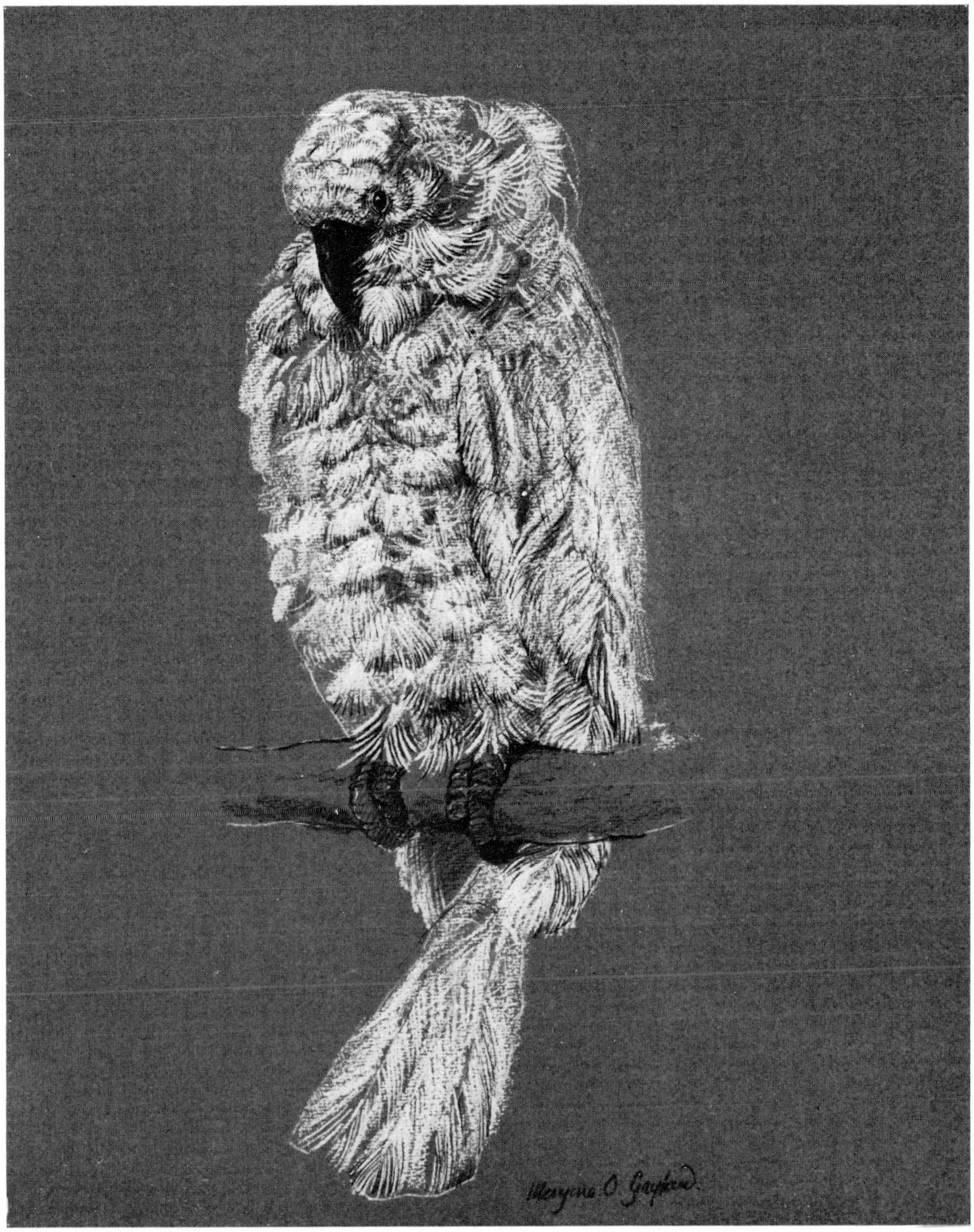

MARJORIE ORPIN GAYLARD
White Cockatoo (Mr. Honey)

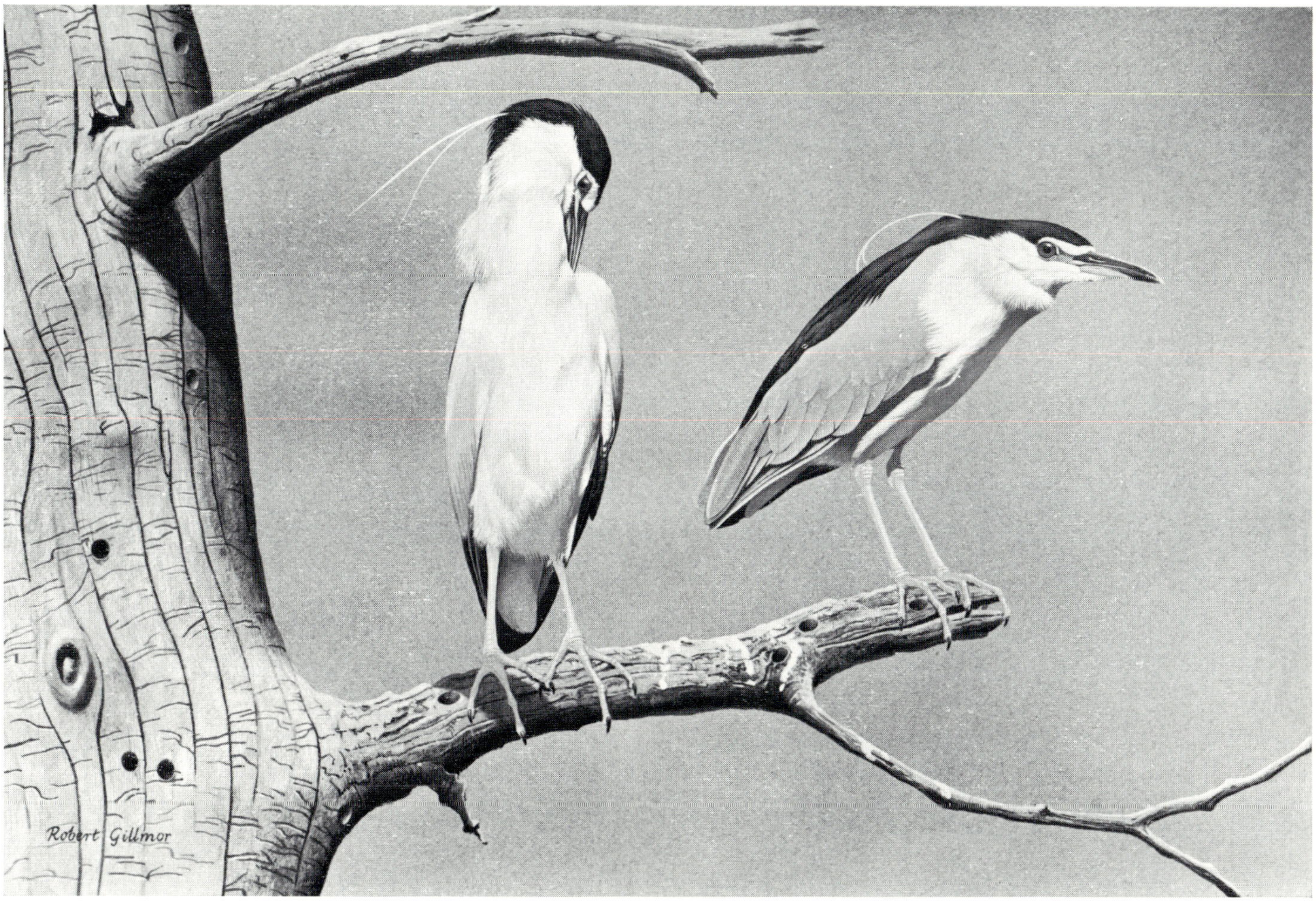

ROBERT GILLMOR
Night Herons

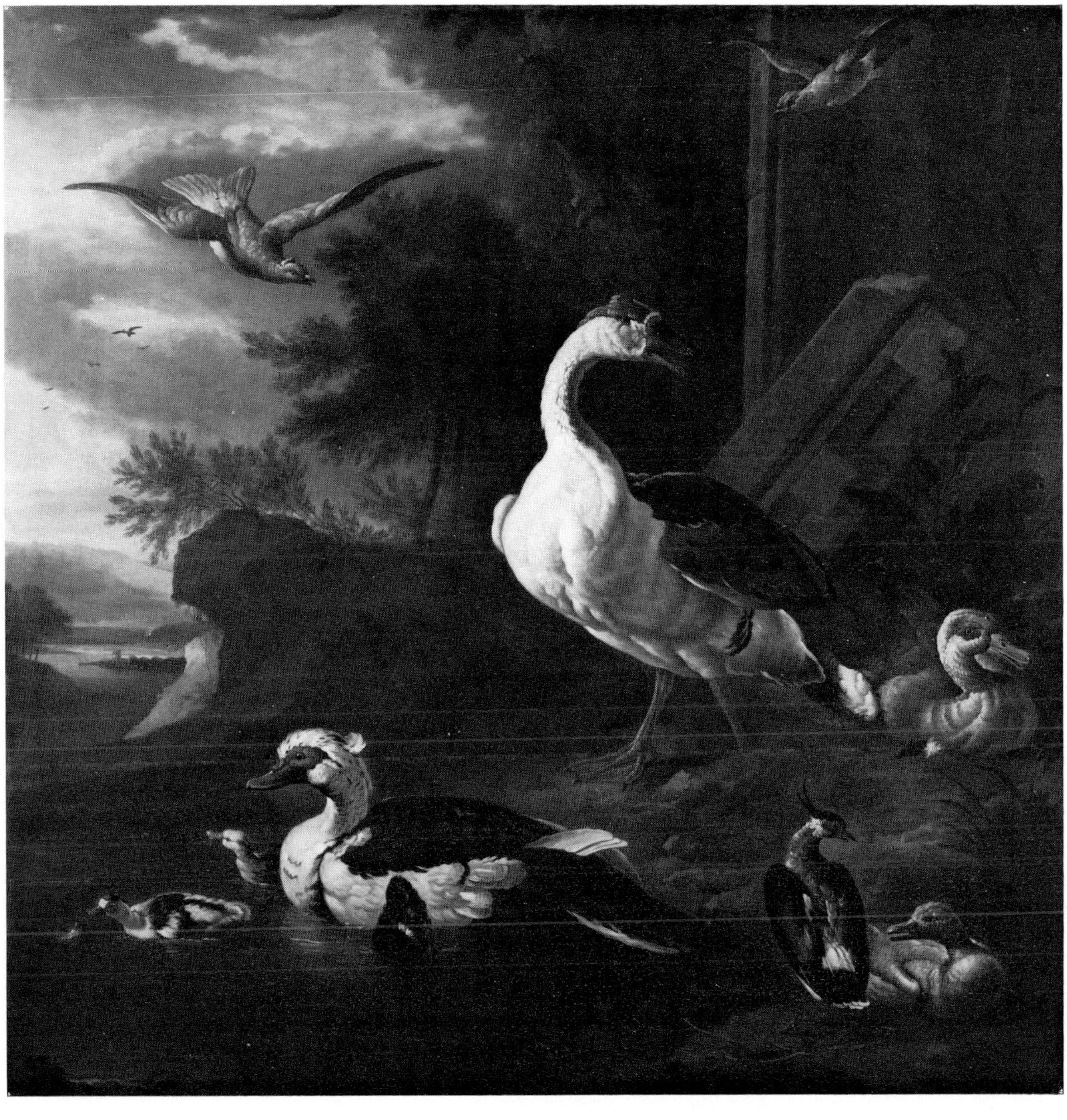

ROBERT GRIFFIER
Egyptian Goose & other African Birds
Courtesy, The Leger Galleries Ltd, London

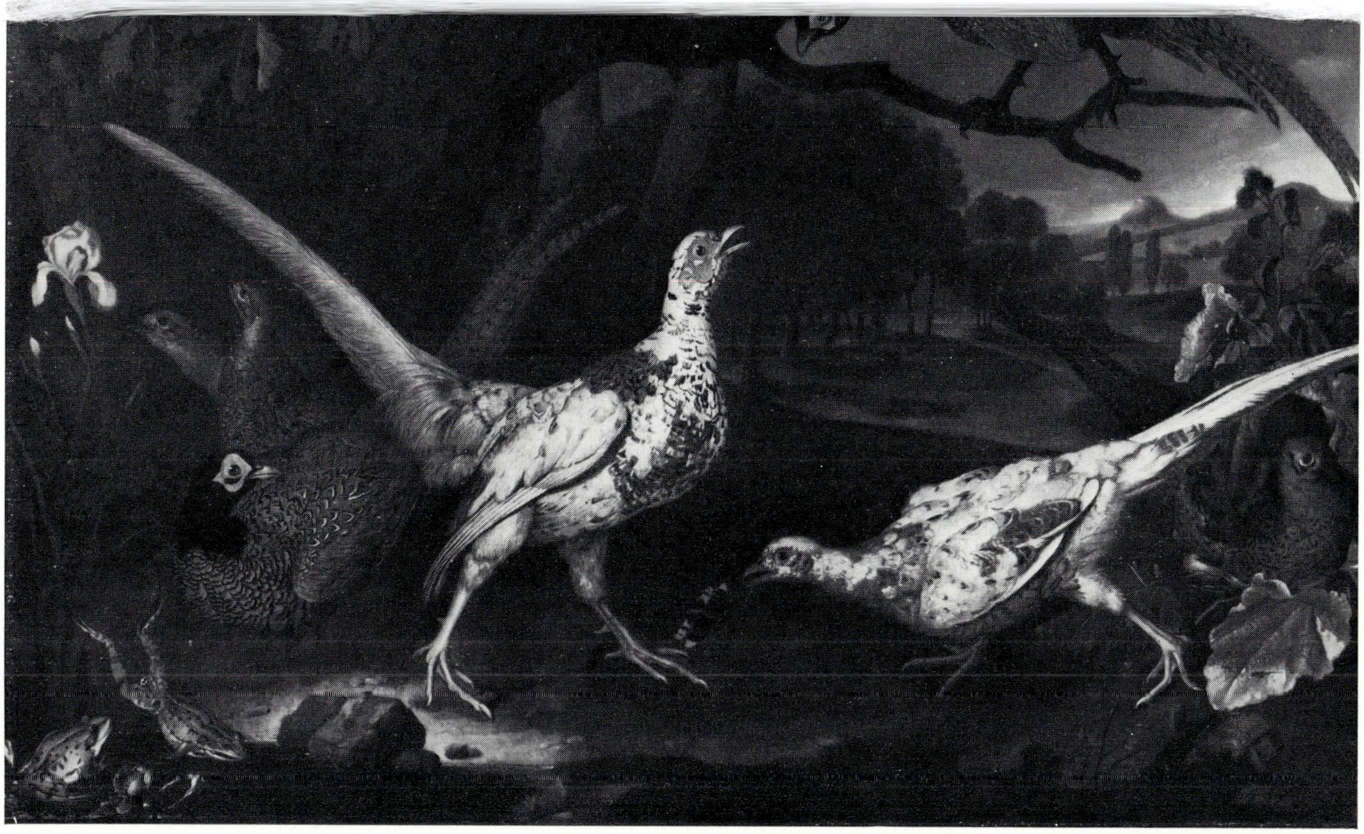

CARL WILHELM DE HAMILTON (or CHARLES WILLIAM)
Pheasants
Courtesy, The Sladmore Gallery, London

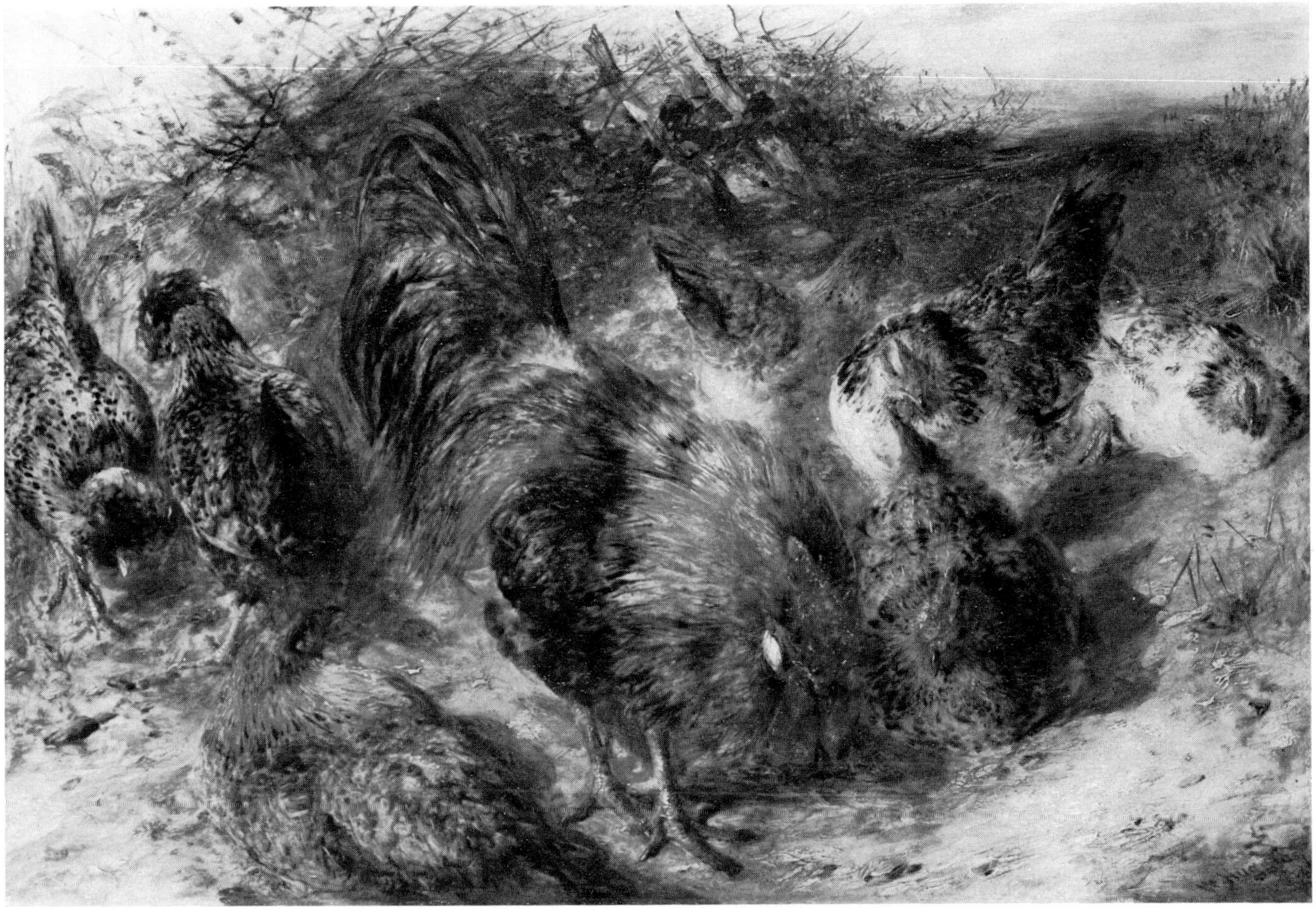

WILLIAM HUGGINS
Chickens
Courtesy, Oscar & Peter Johnson Ltd, London

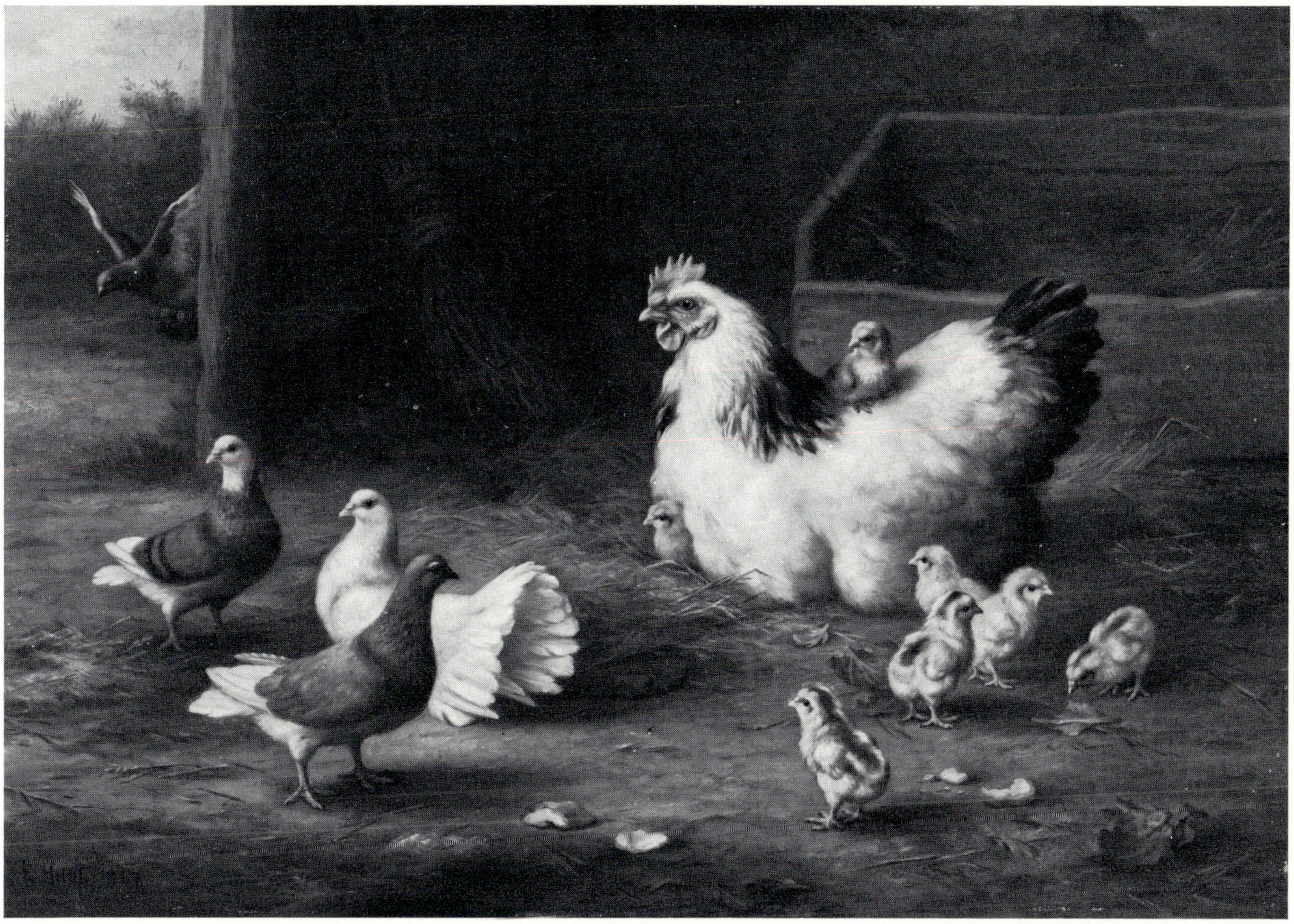

EDGAR HUNT
Hens & Pigeons
Courtesy, Spencer S.A., London

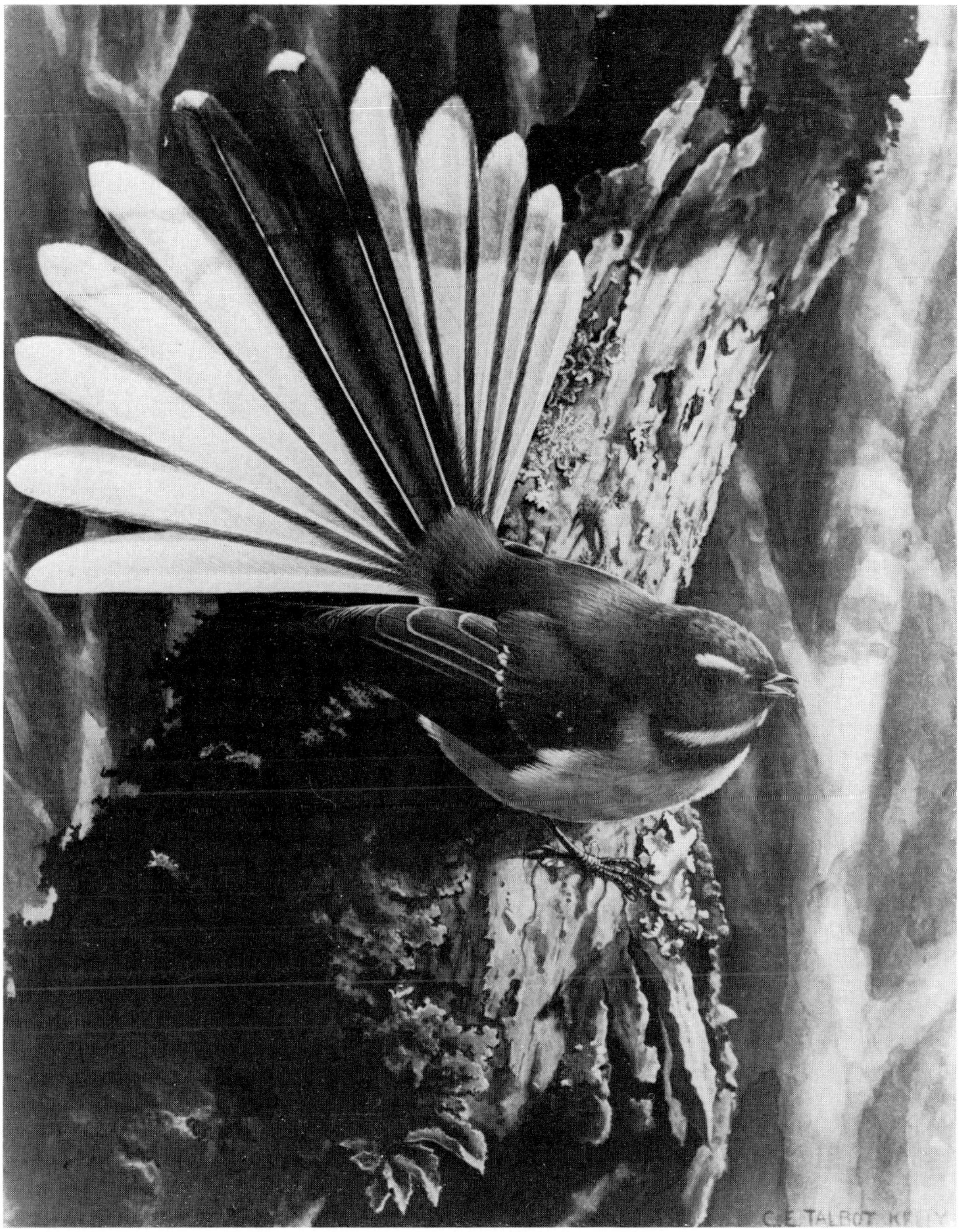

CHLOE E. TALBOT KELLY
New Zealand Fantail

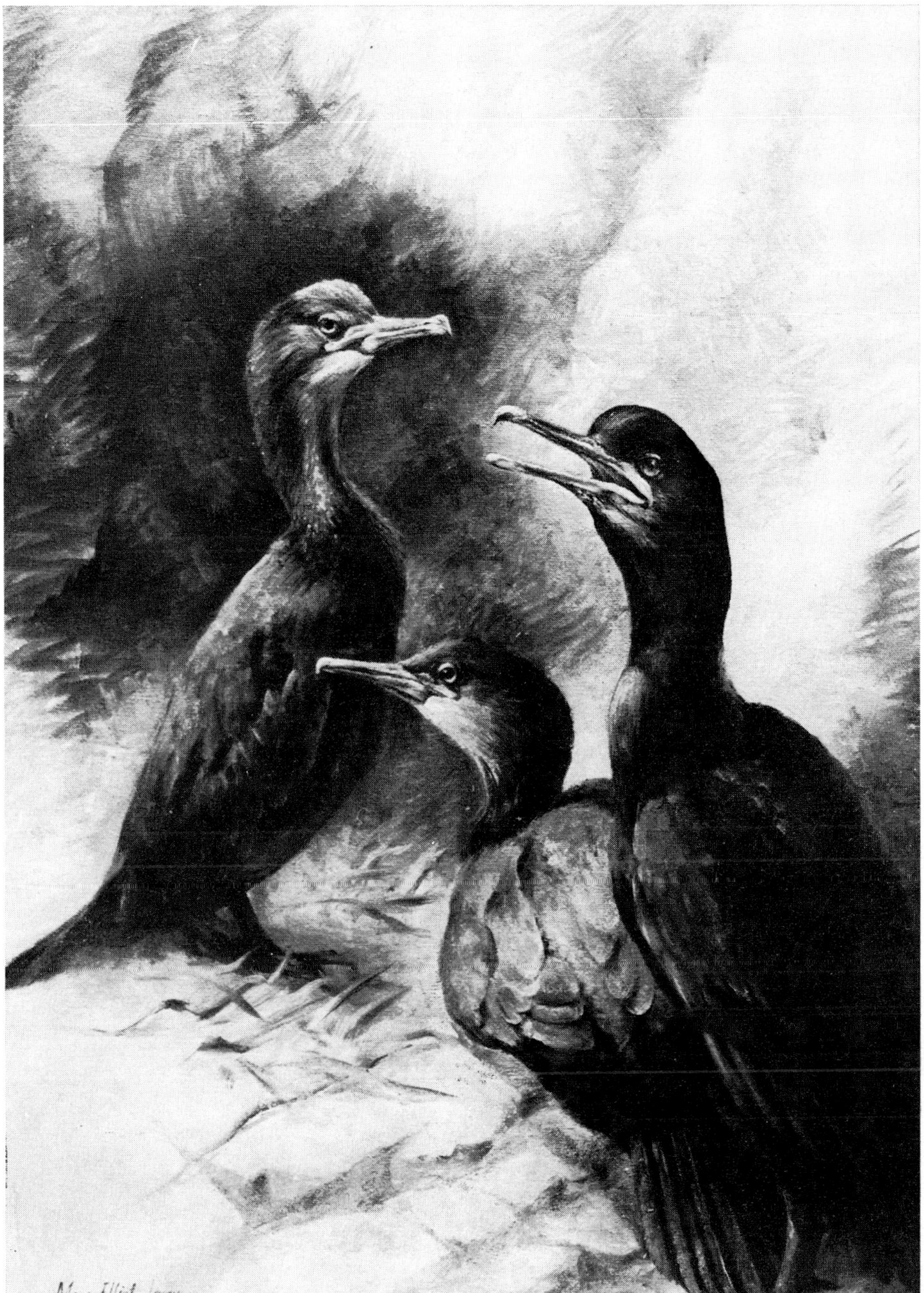

MARY ELLIOT LACEY
Shag

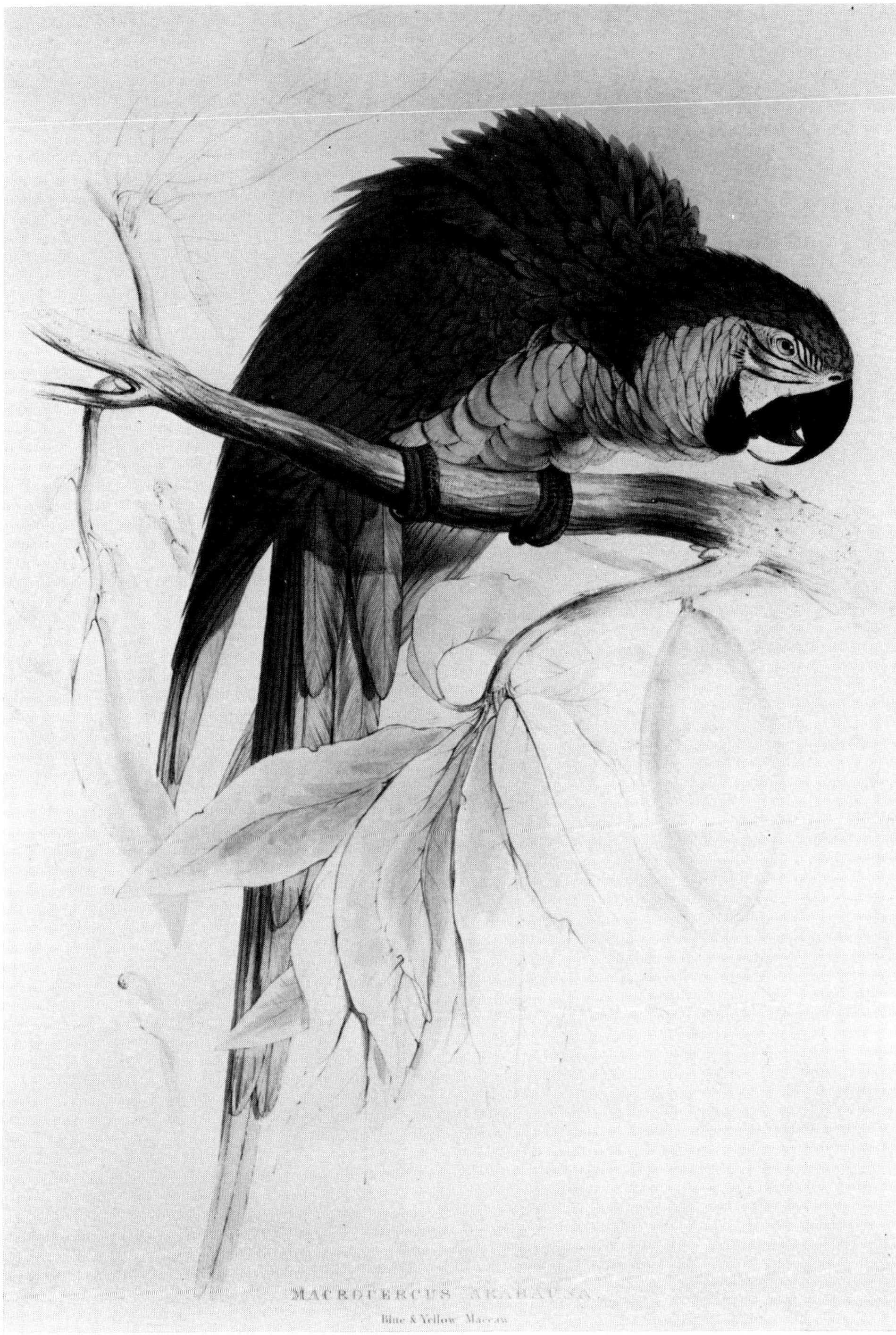

EDWARD LEAR
Blue & Yellow Macaw
Courtesy, Hazlitt, Gooden & Fox Ltd, London

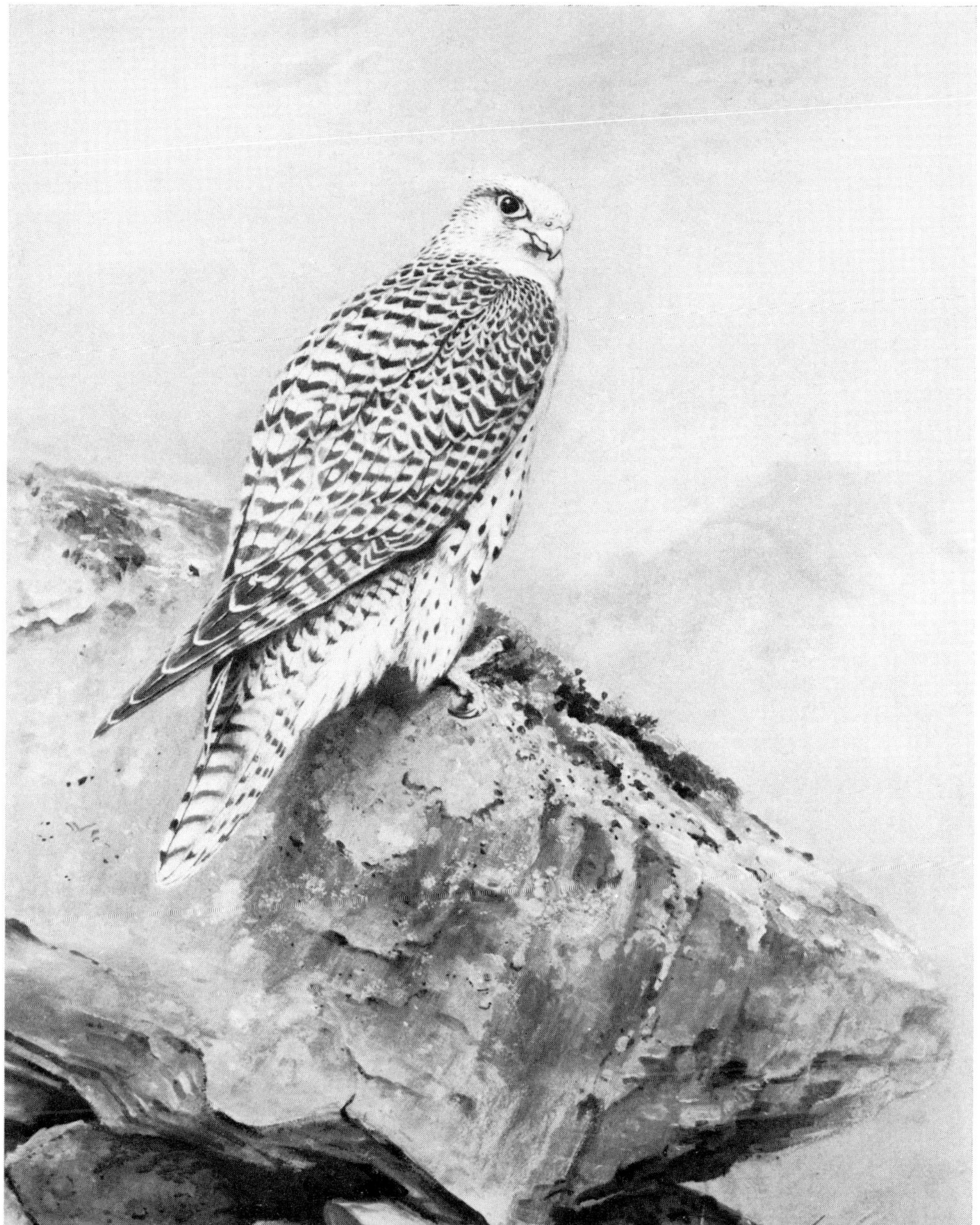

GEORGE E. LODGE
Gyr Falcon
Courtesy, The Tryon Gallery Ltd, London

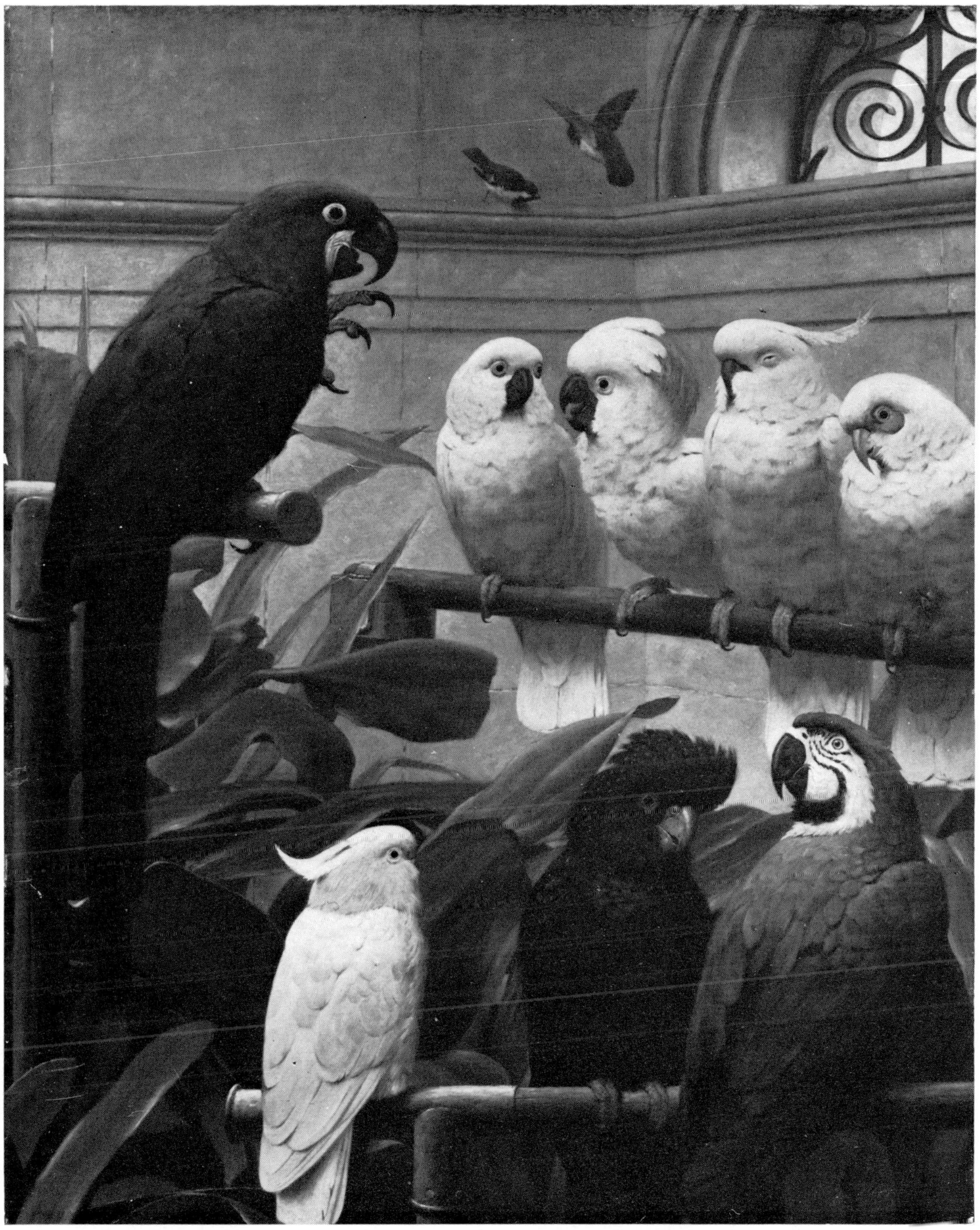

HENRY STACY MARKS
'A Select Committee'
Courtesy, Walker Art Gallery, Liverpool

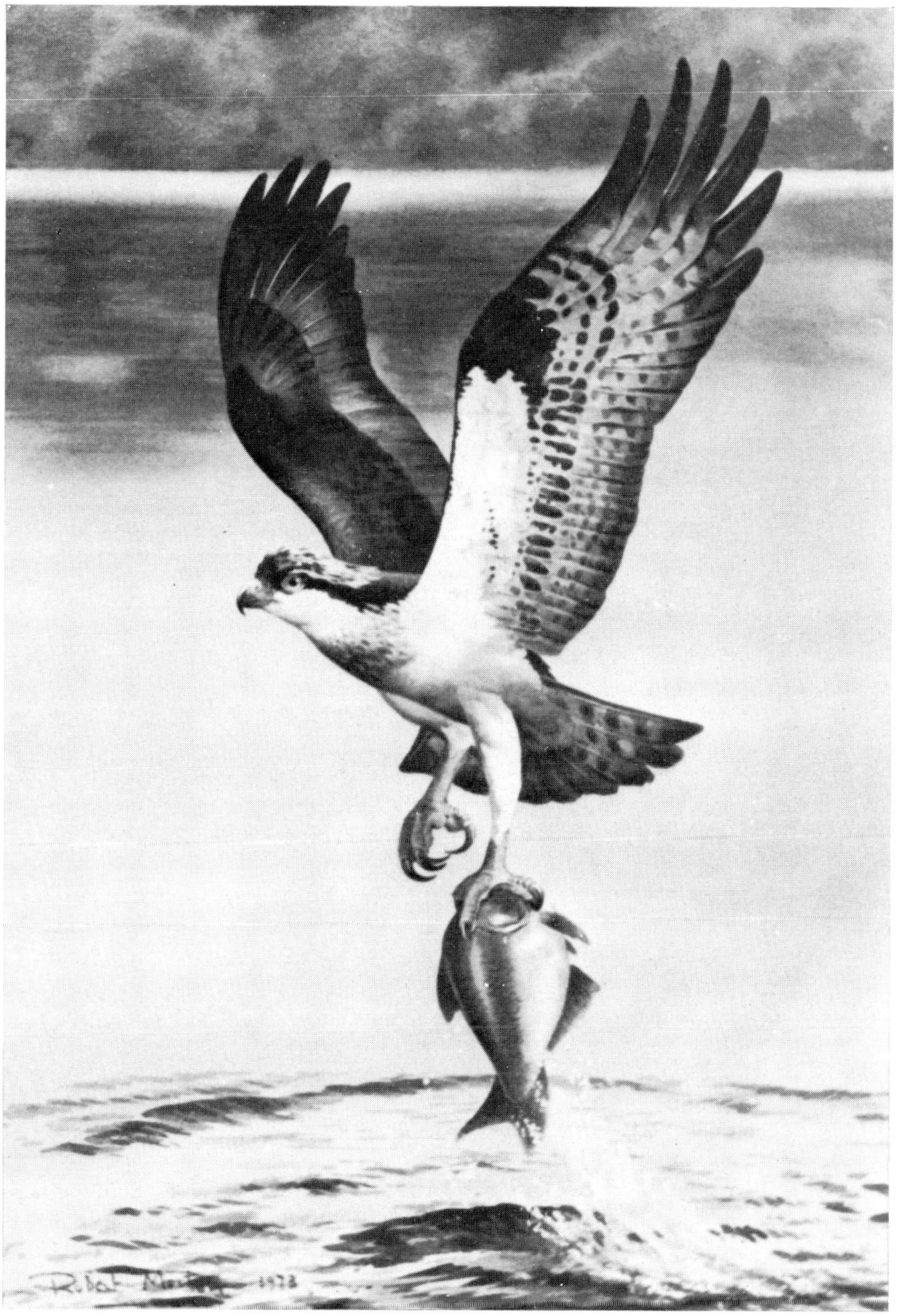

MICHAEL ROBERT MORTON
Osprey

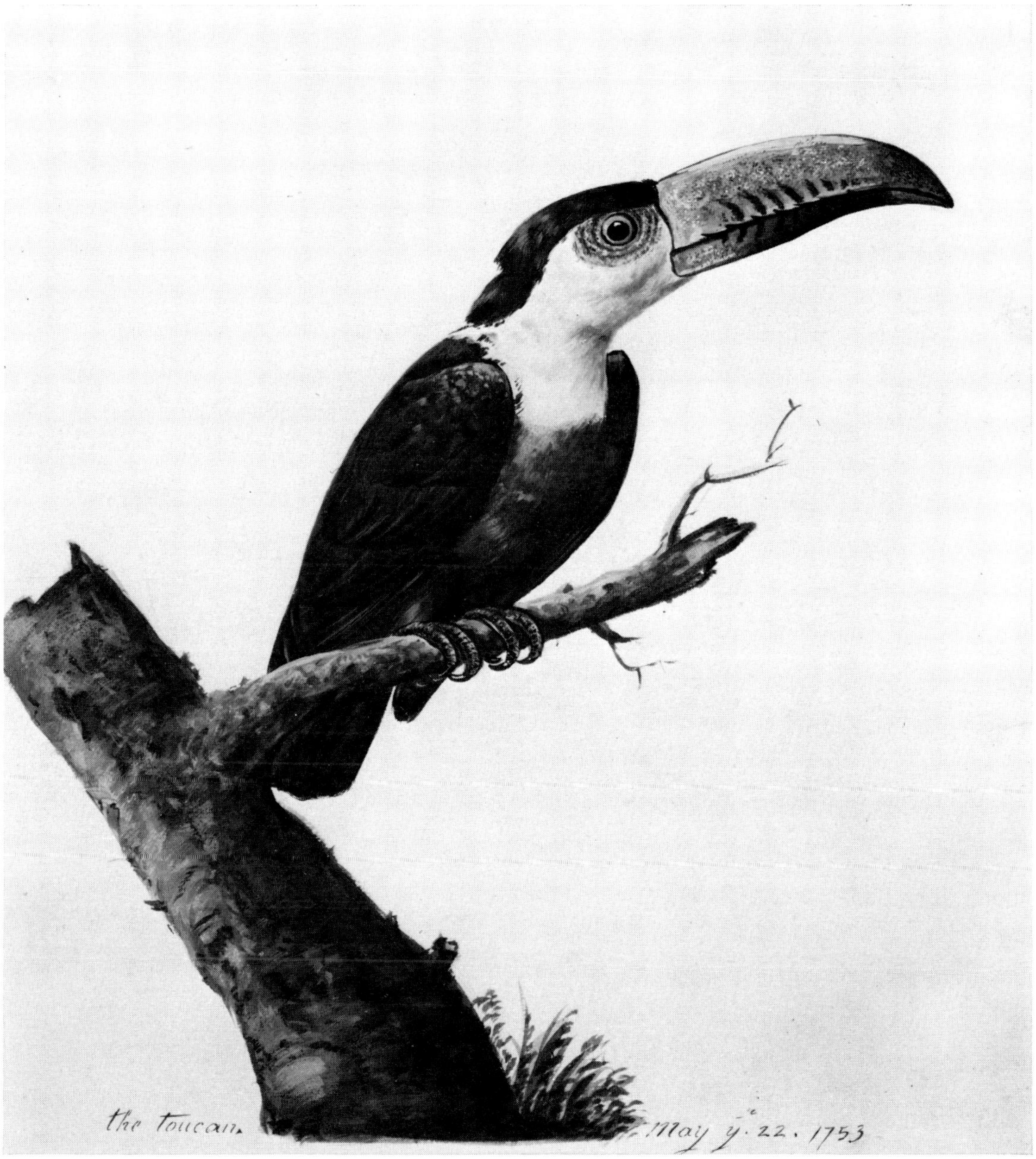

PETER PAILLON
The Toucan
Courtesy, Spink & Son Ltd, London

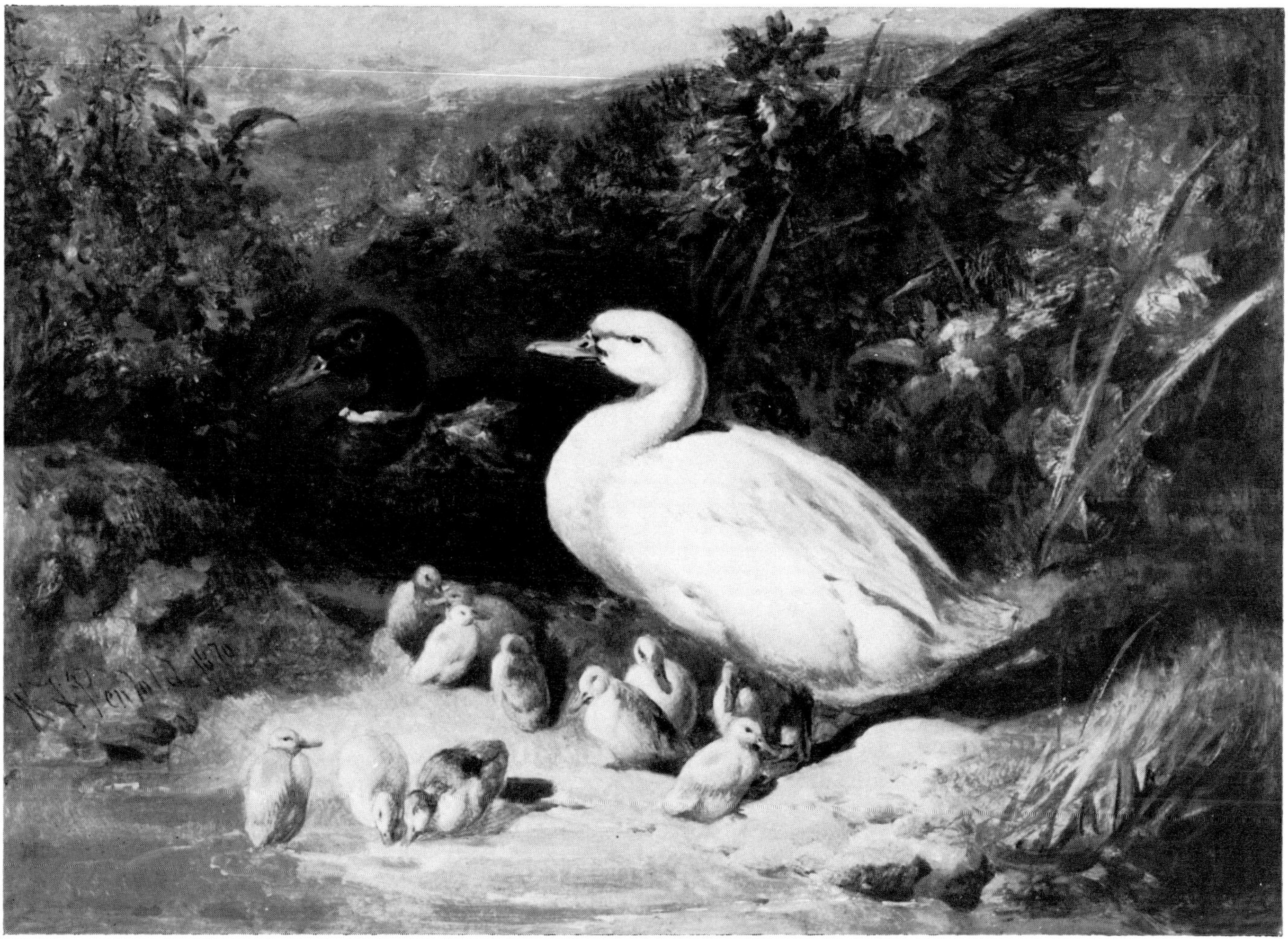

W. F. PENFOLD
Ducks & Ducklings
Courtesy, Oscar & Peter Johnson Ltd, London

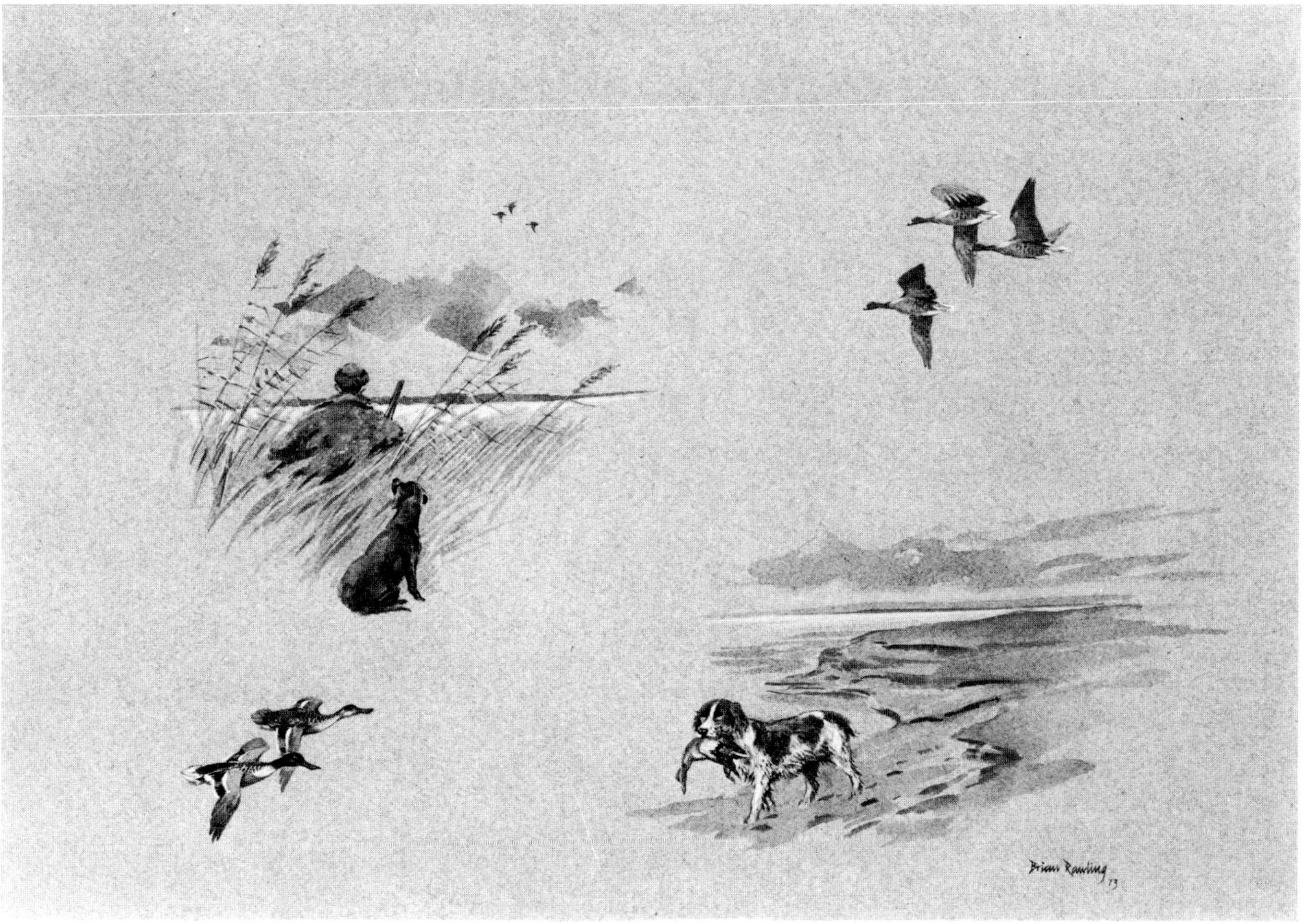

BRIAN RAWLING
The Wild-Fowler
Courtesy, The Macdonald Booth Gallery, London

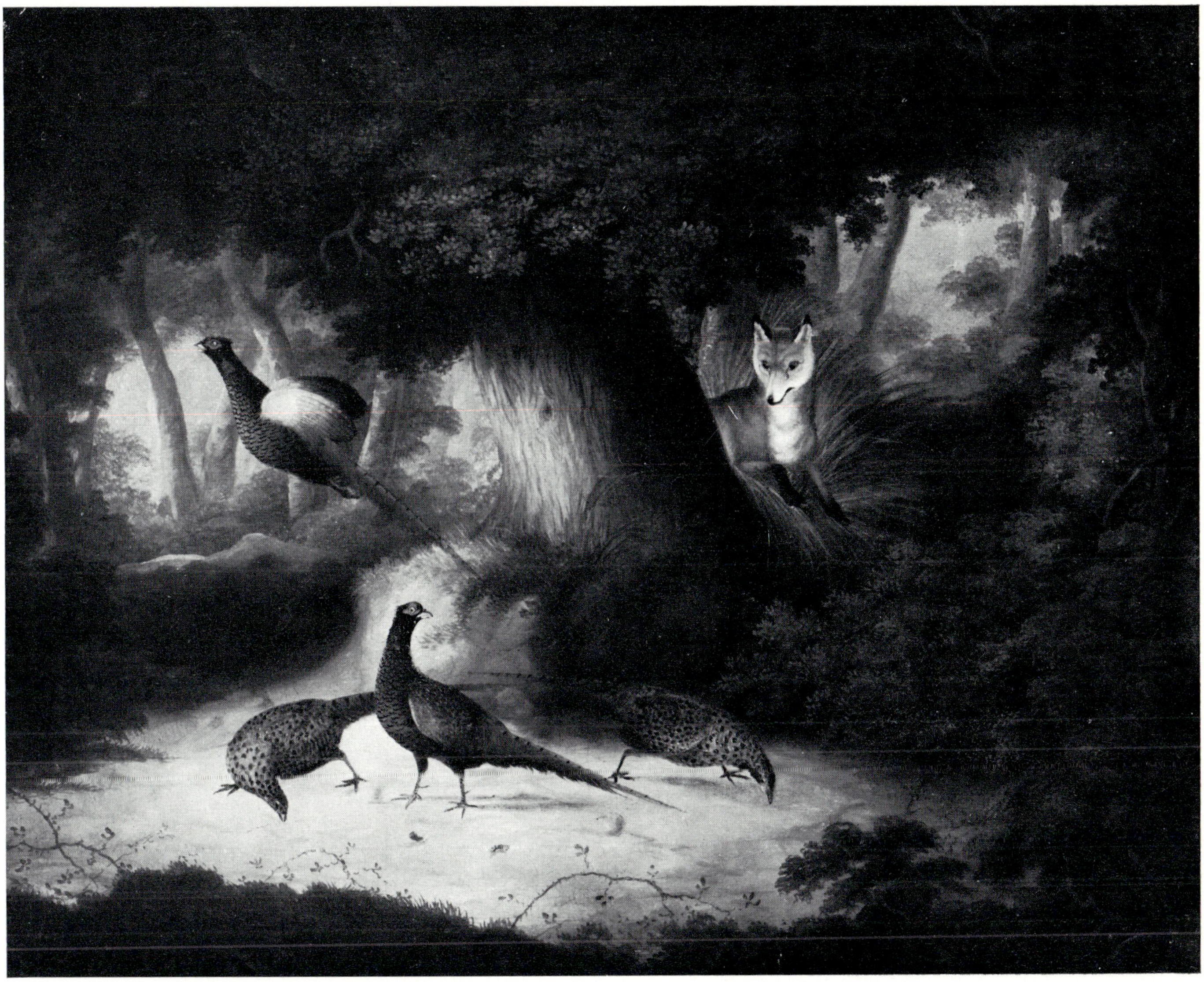

PHILIP REINAGLE
'Disturbed'
Courtesy, The Moorland Gallery Ltd, London

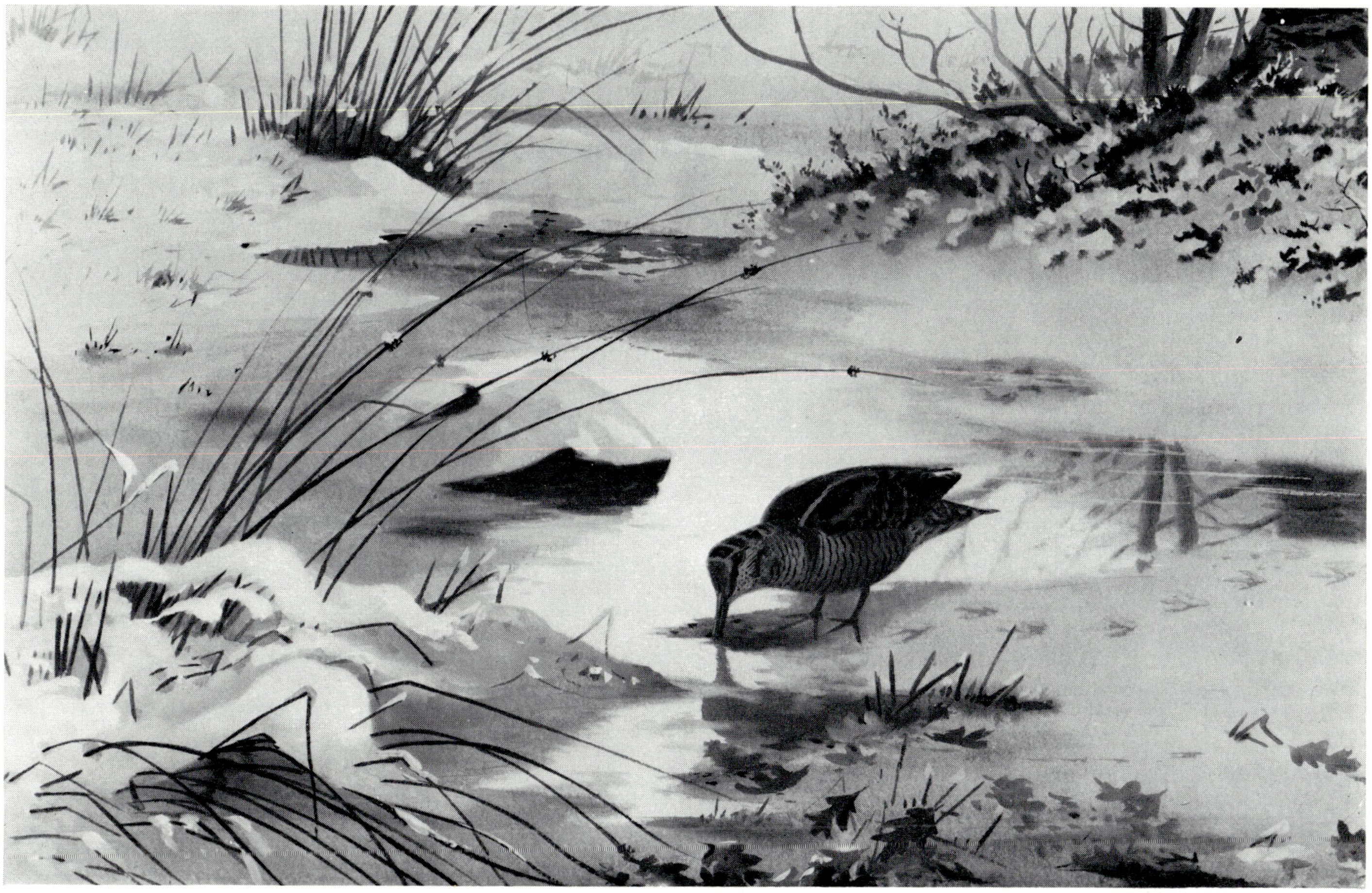

PHILIP RICKMAN
Woodcock
Courtesy, The Tryon Gallery Ltd, London

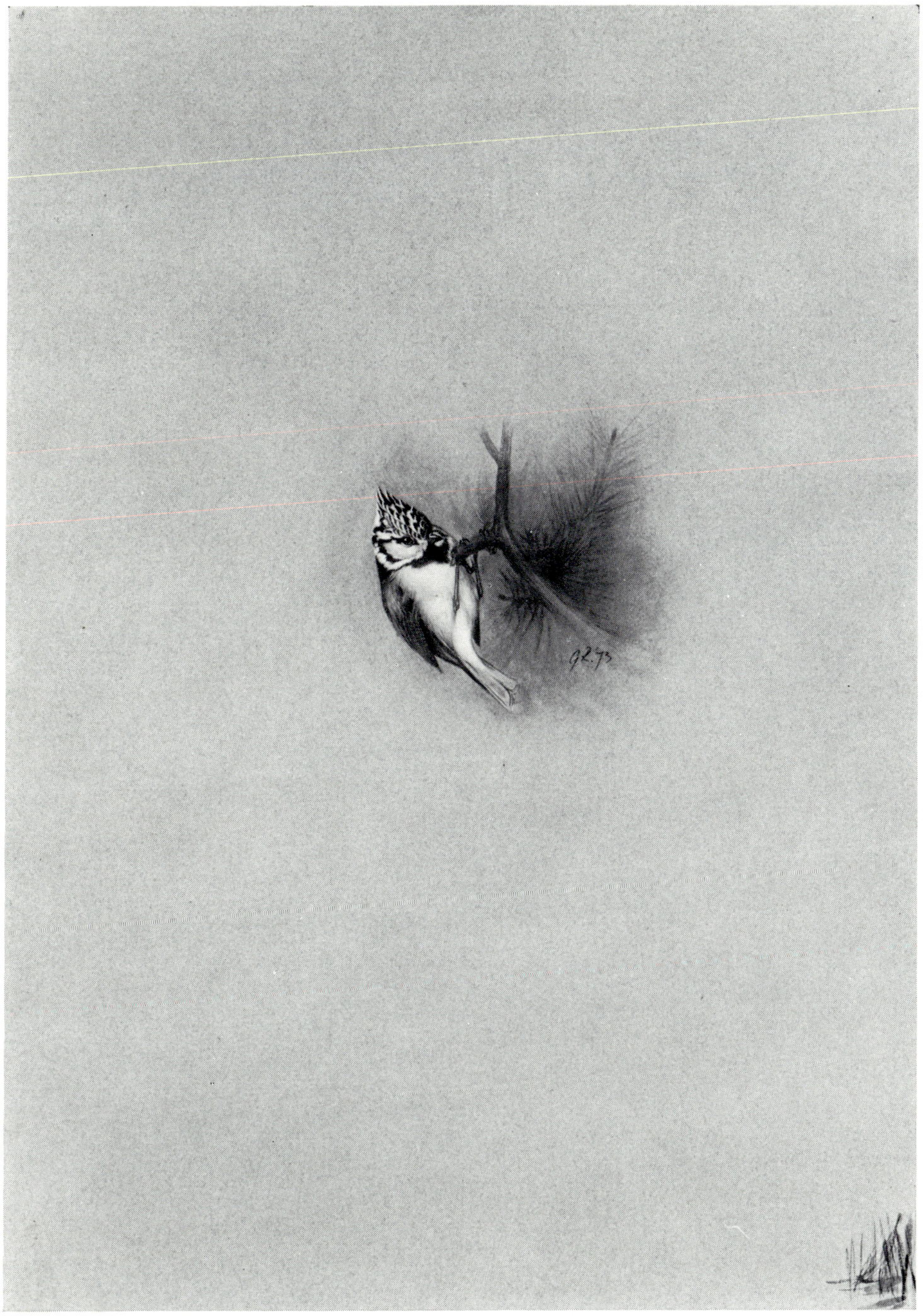

GEORGE ROE
Crested Tit on a Pine Branch
Courtesy, The Macdonald Booth Gallery, London

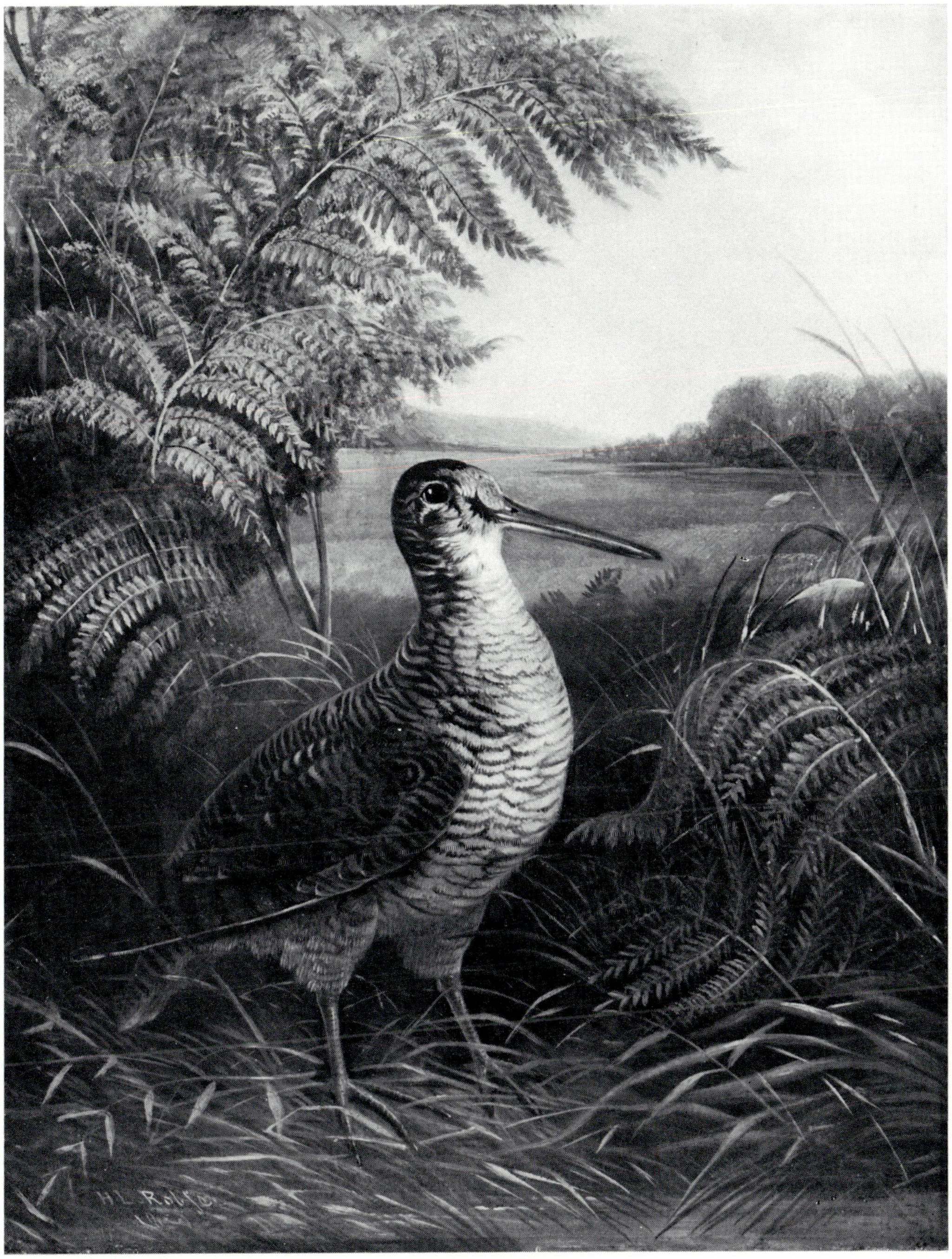

HENRY LEONIDES ROLFE
Woodcock
Courtesy, B. Cohen & Sons, London

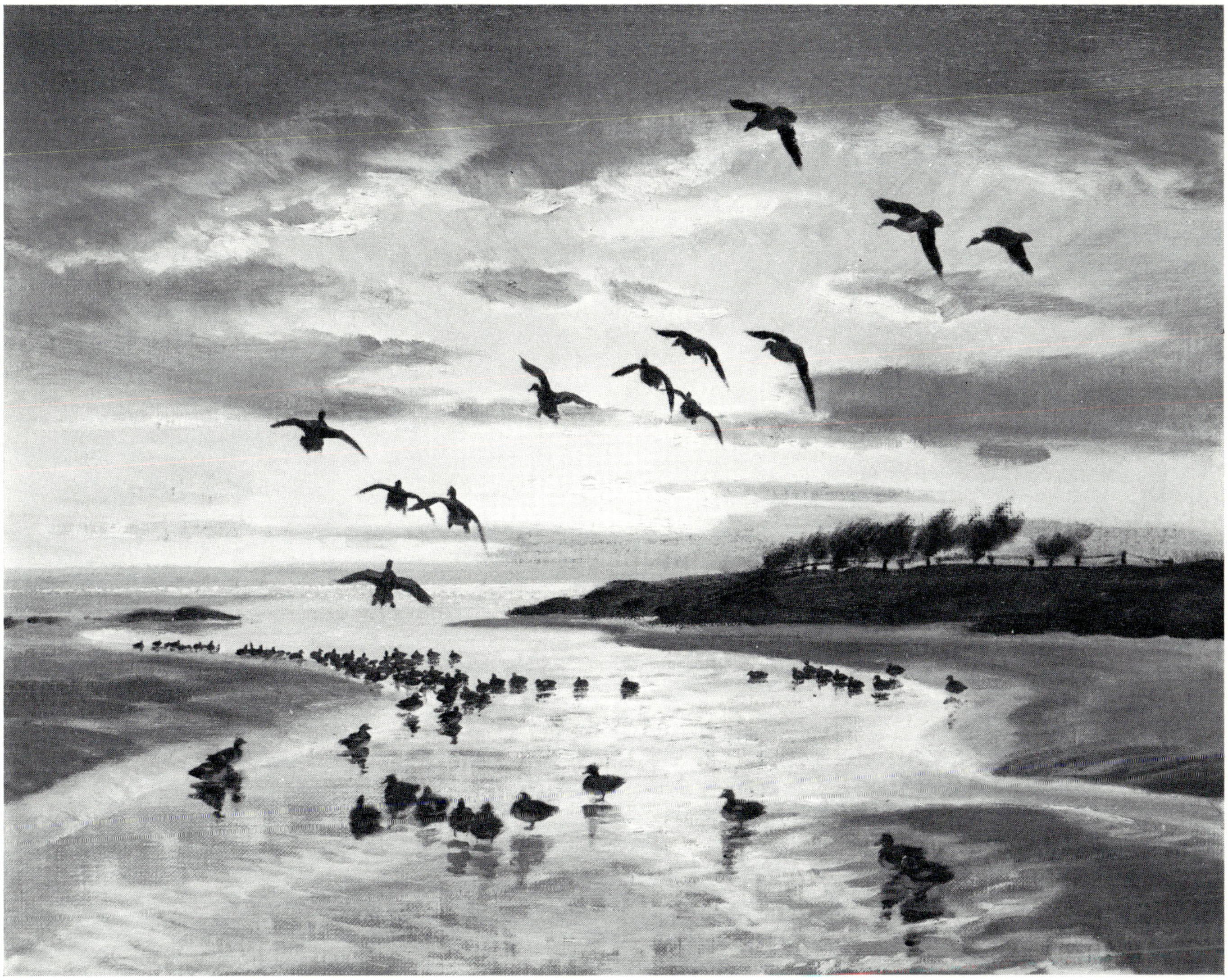

SIR PETER SCOTT
Teal coming in at low tide
Courtesy, Arthur Ackermann & Son Ltd, London

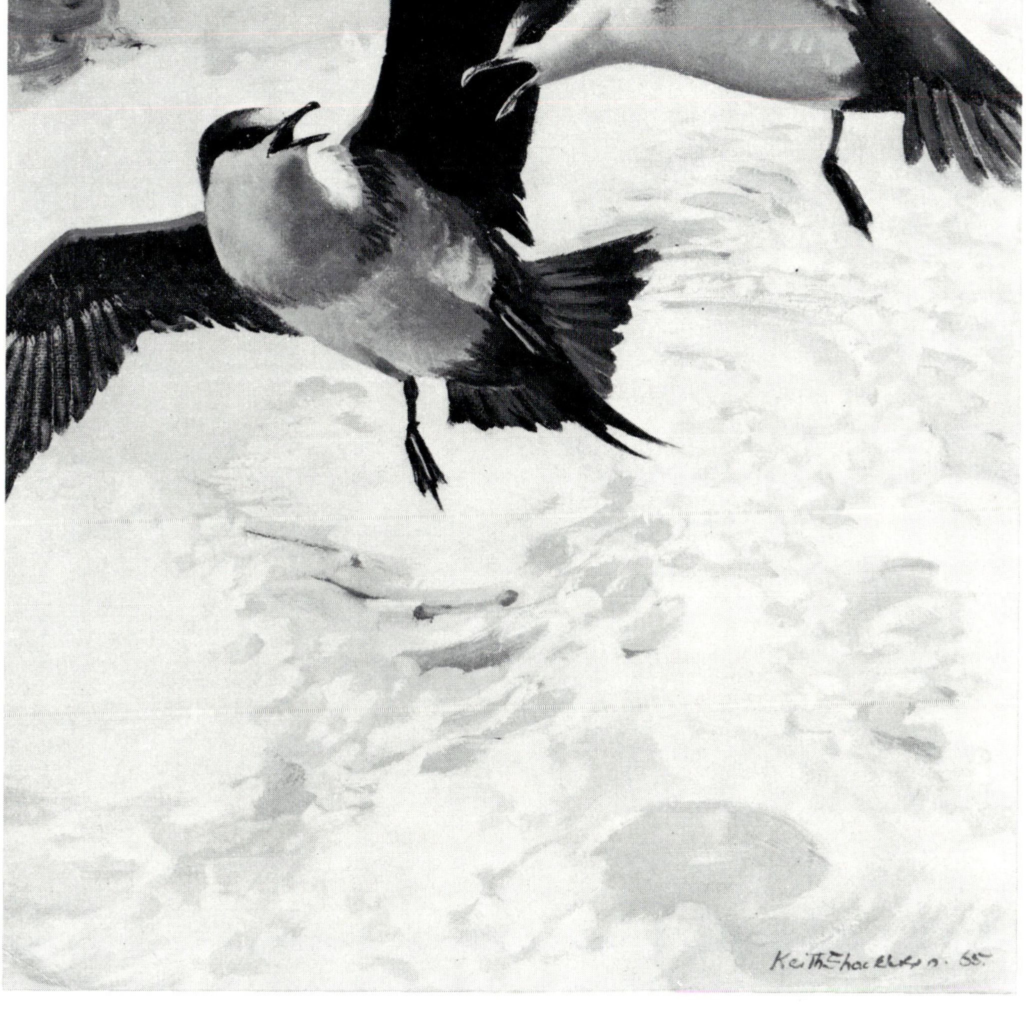

KEITH SHACKLETON
Arctic Skuas

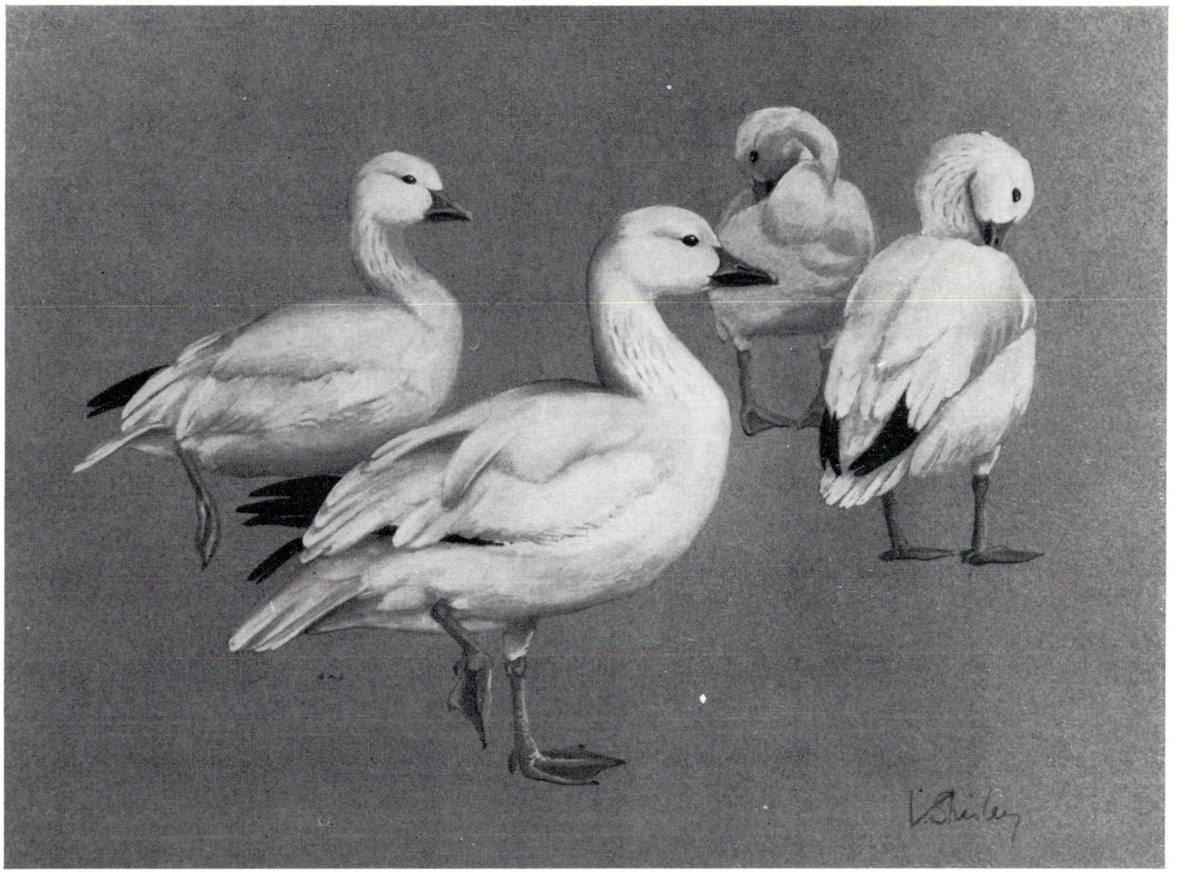

VALERIE SHIRLEY
Greater Snow Geese
Courtesy, The Sladmore Gallery, London

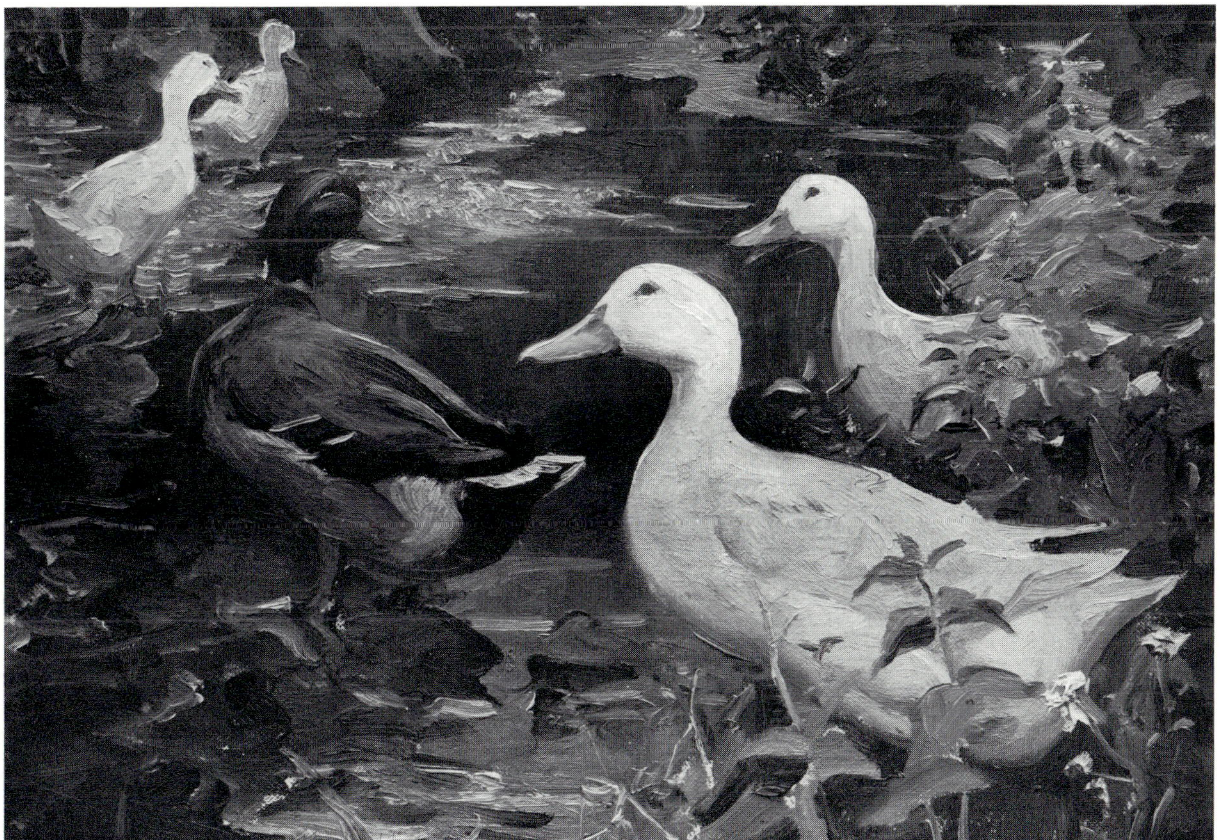

CHARLES W. SIMPSON
Crossing the stream

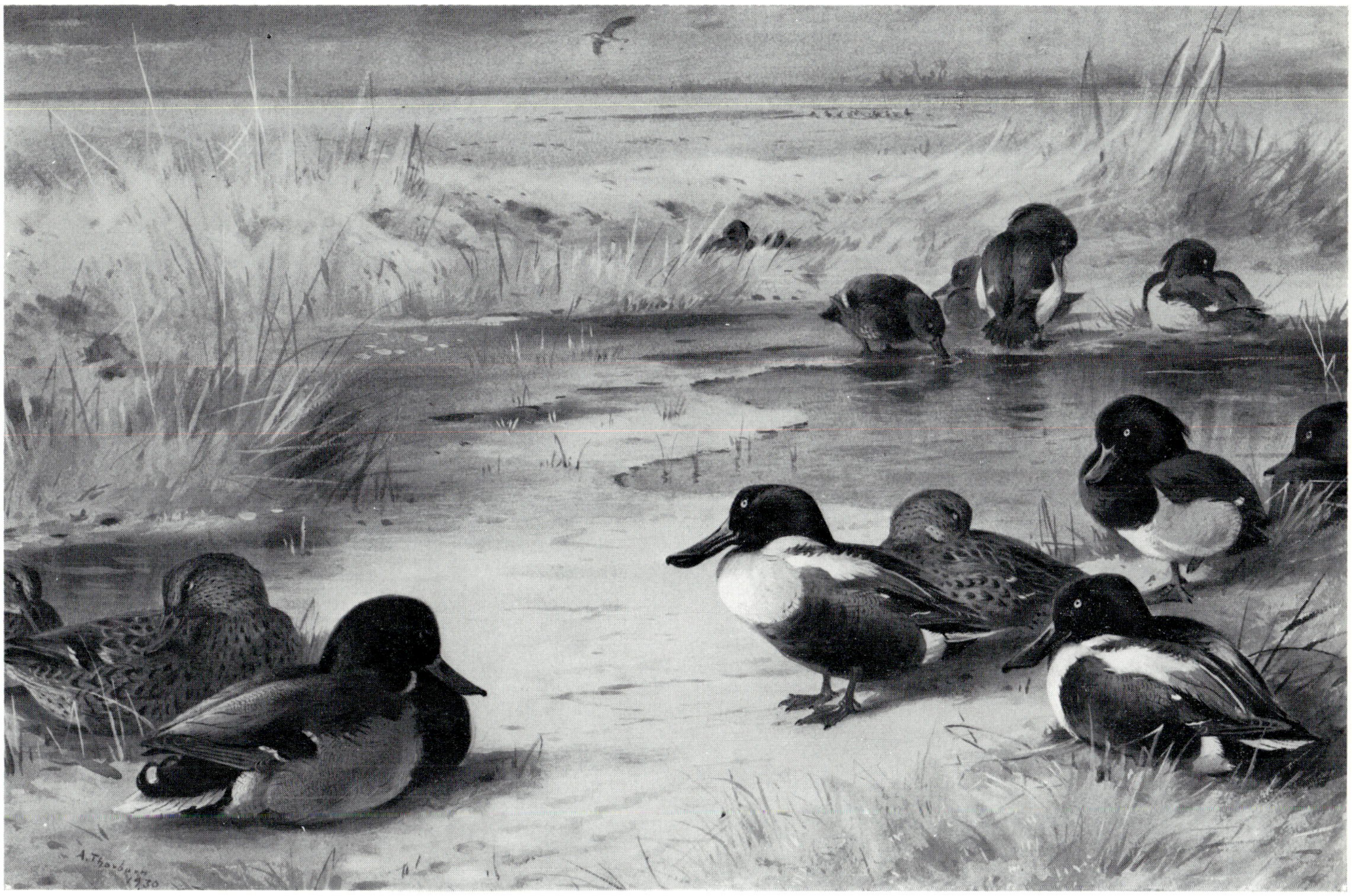

ARCHIBALD THORBURN, F.Z.S.
The Frosty Marshes S & D 1930
Courtesy, The Macdonald Booth Gallery, London

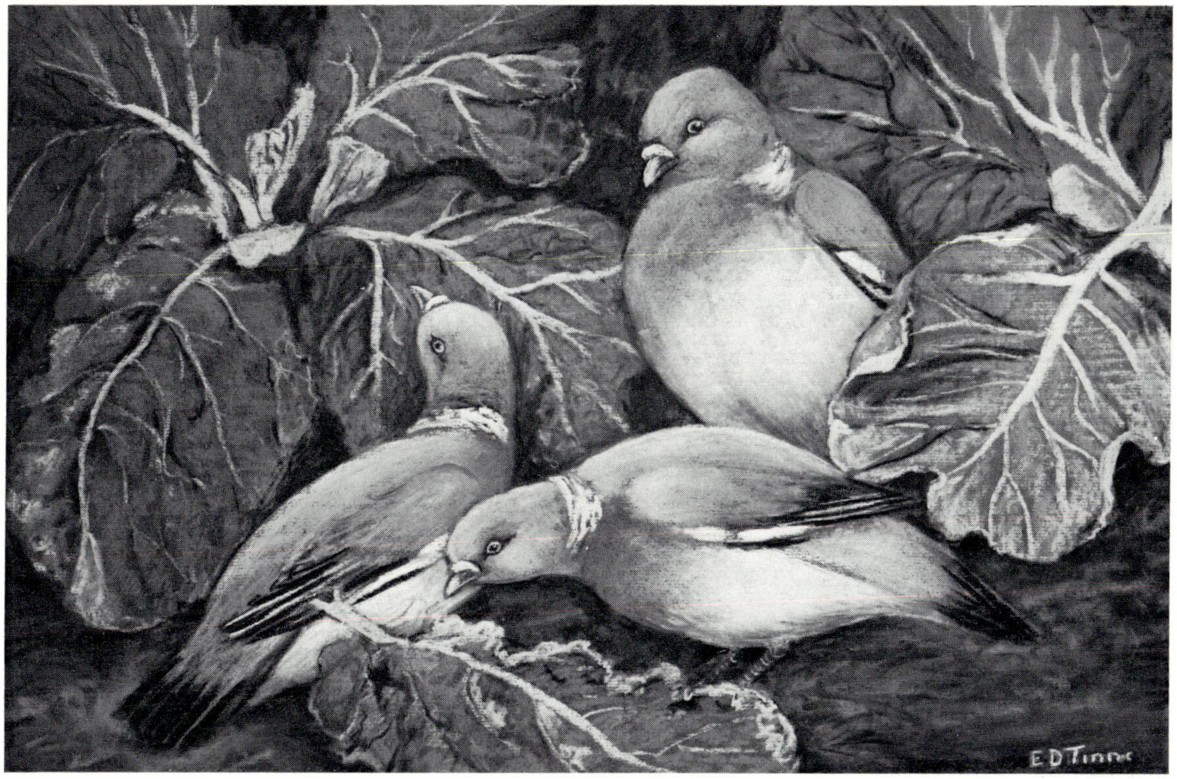

DOROTHEA TINNE
'Spring Cabbages'

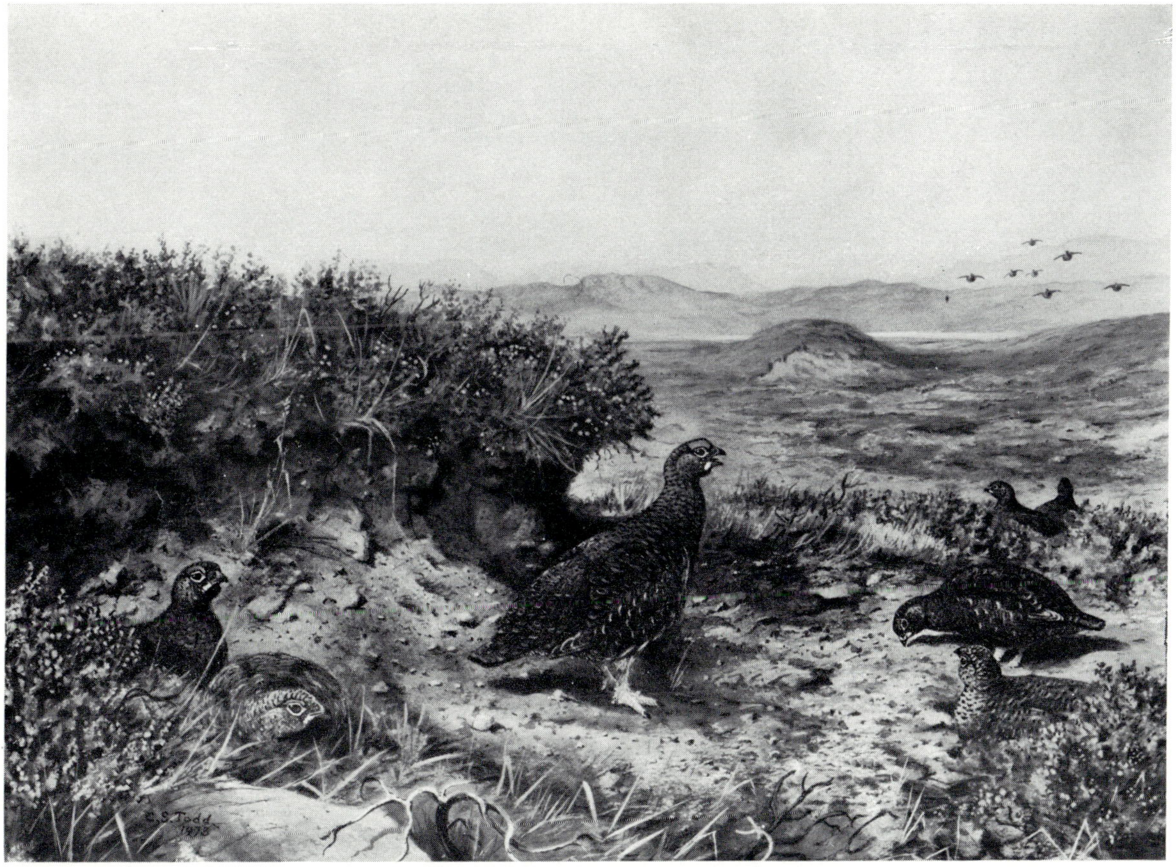

CHARLES STANLEY TODD
Grouse
Courtesy, John Moncrieff Macmillan Gallery, Perth

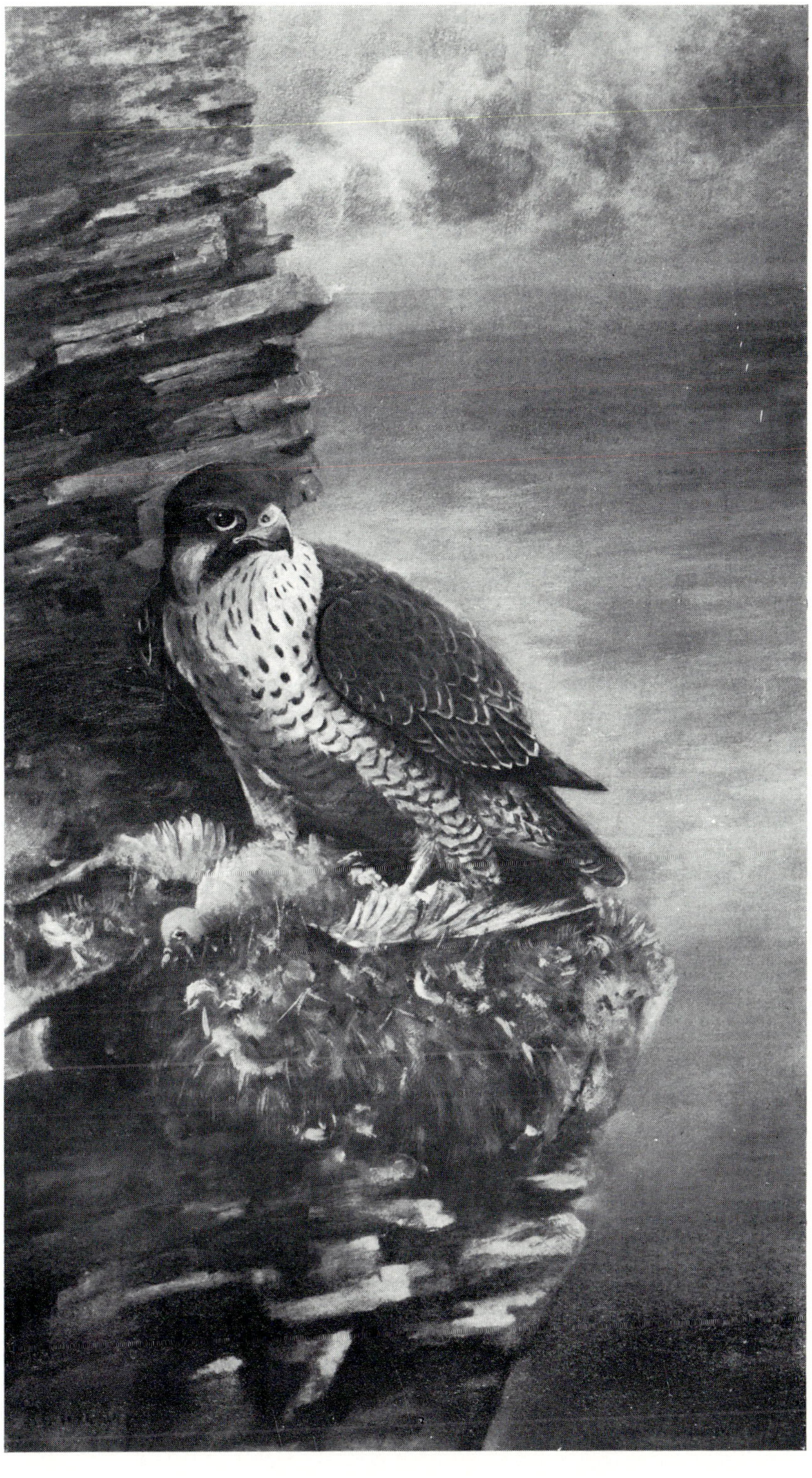

RICHARD BARRIE TRELEAVEN
Peregrin Falcon on a Kill, North Cornwall

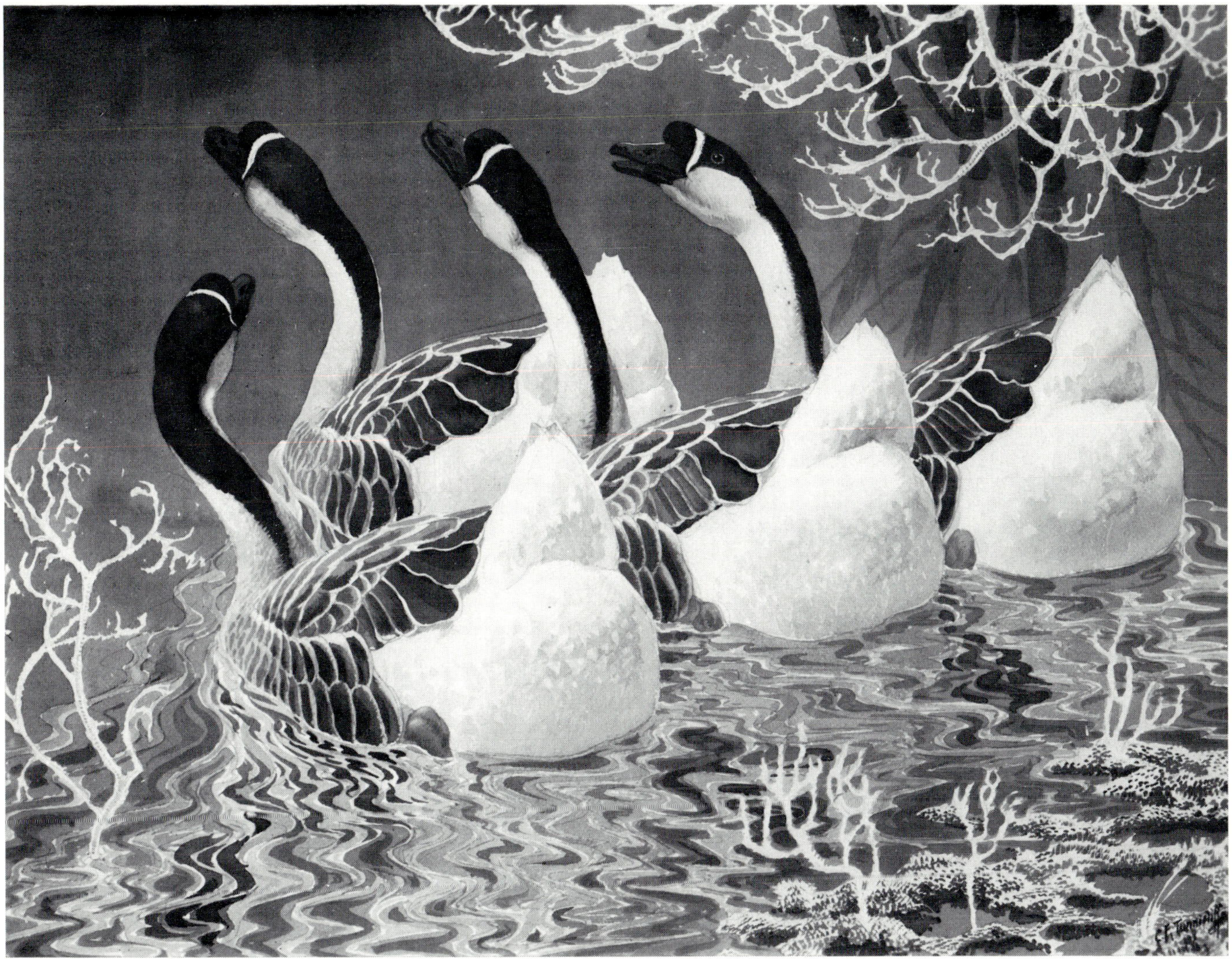

CHARLES FREDERICK TUNNICLIFFE
'Four Chinese

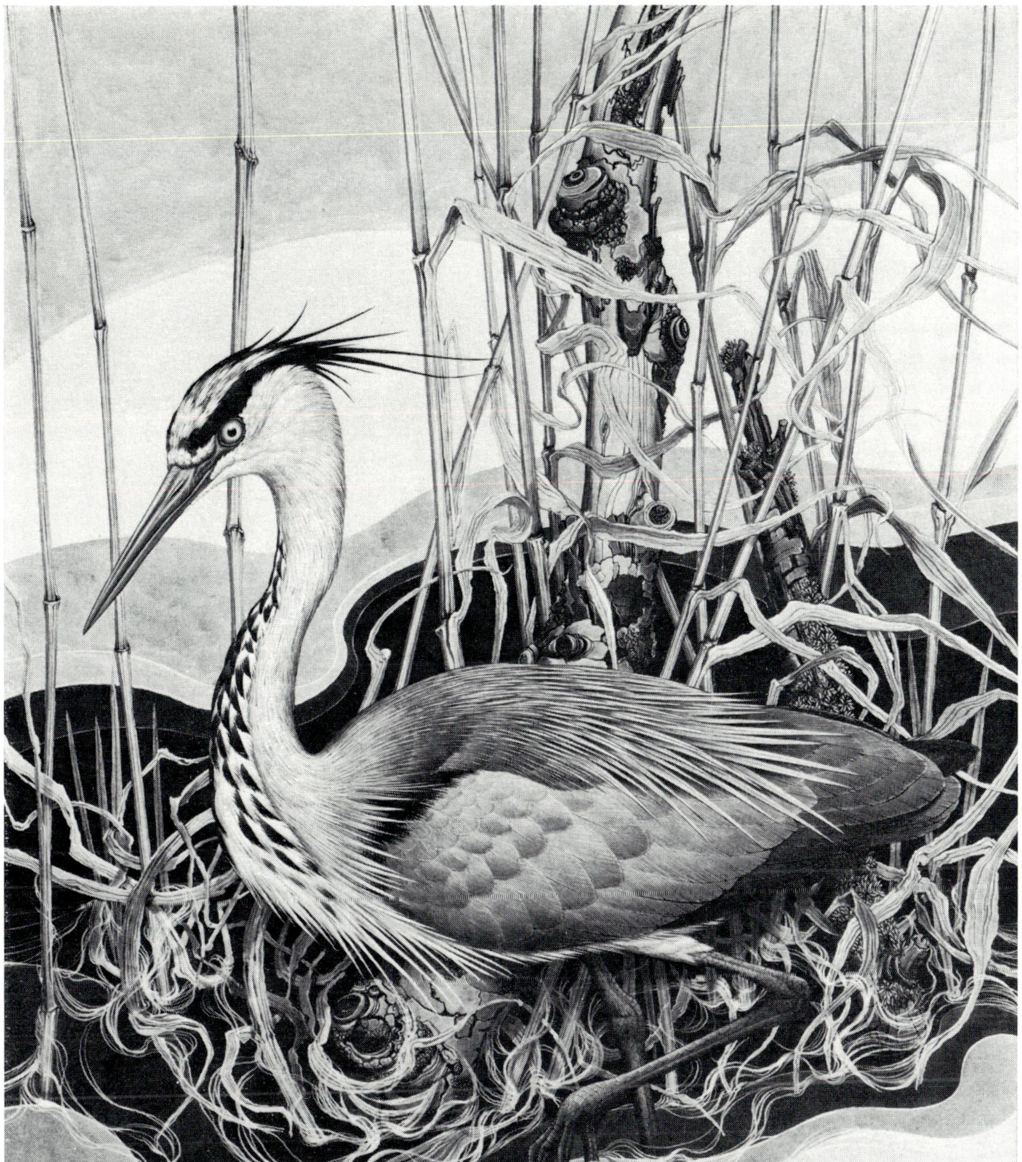

MICHAEL WARREN
Grey Heron

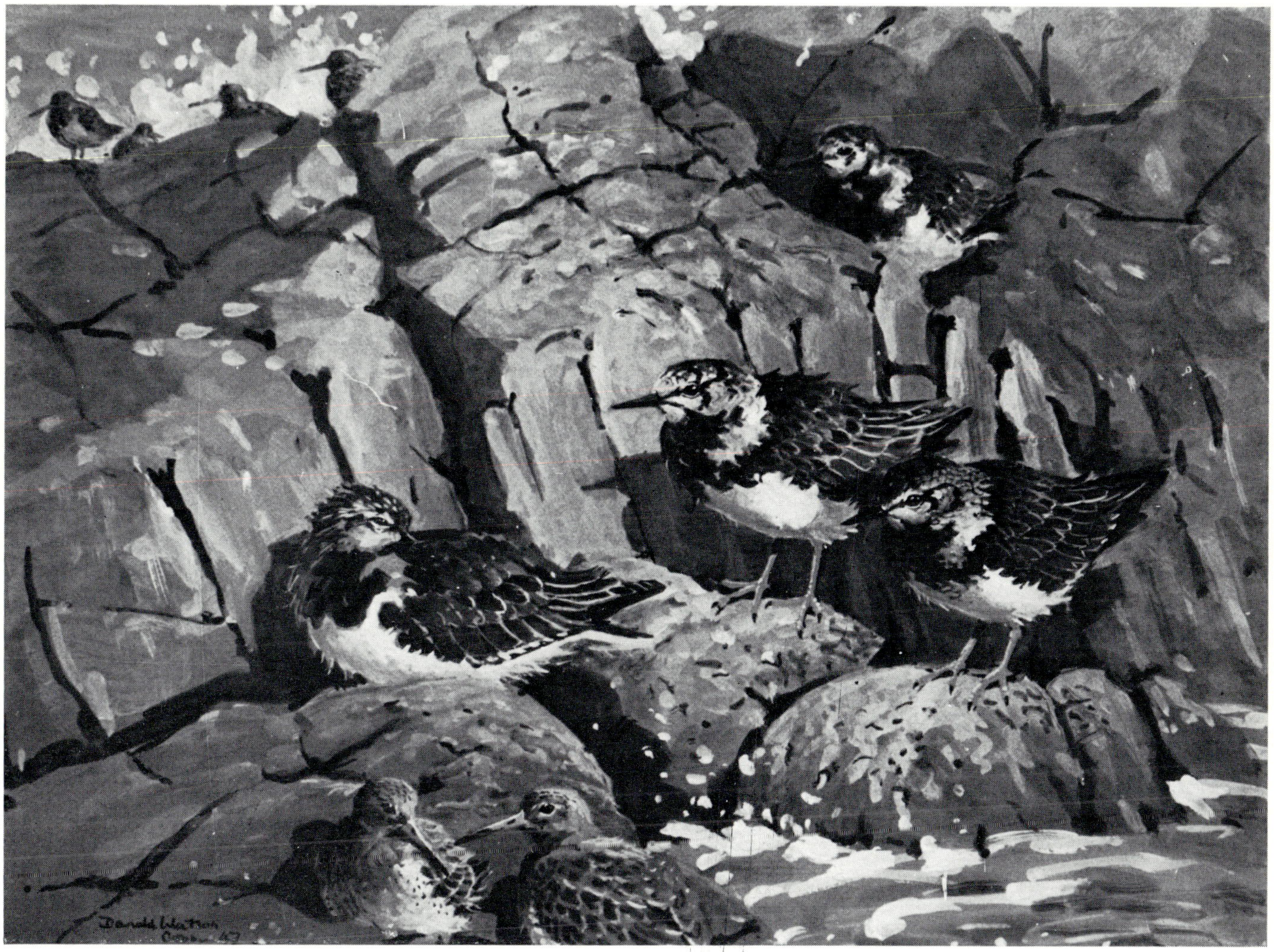

DONALD WATSON
Turnstones and Purple Sandpipers – Isle of May

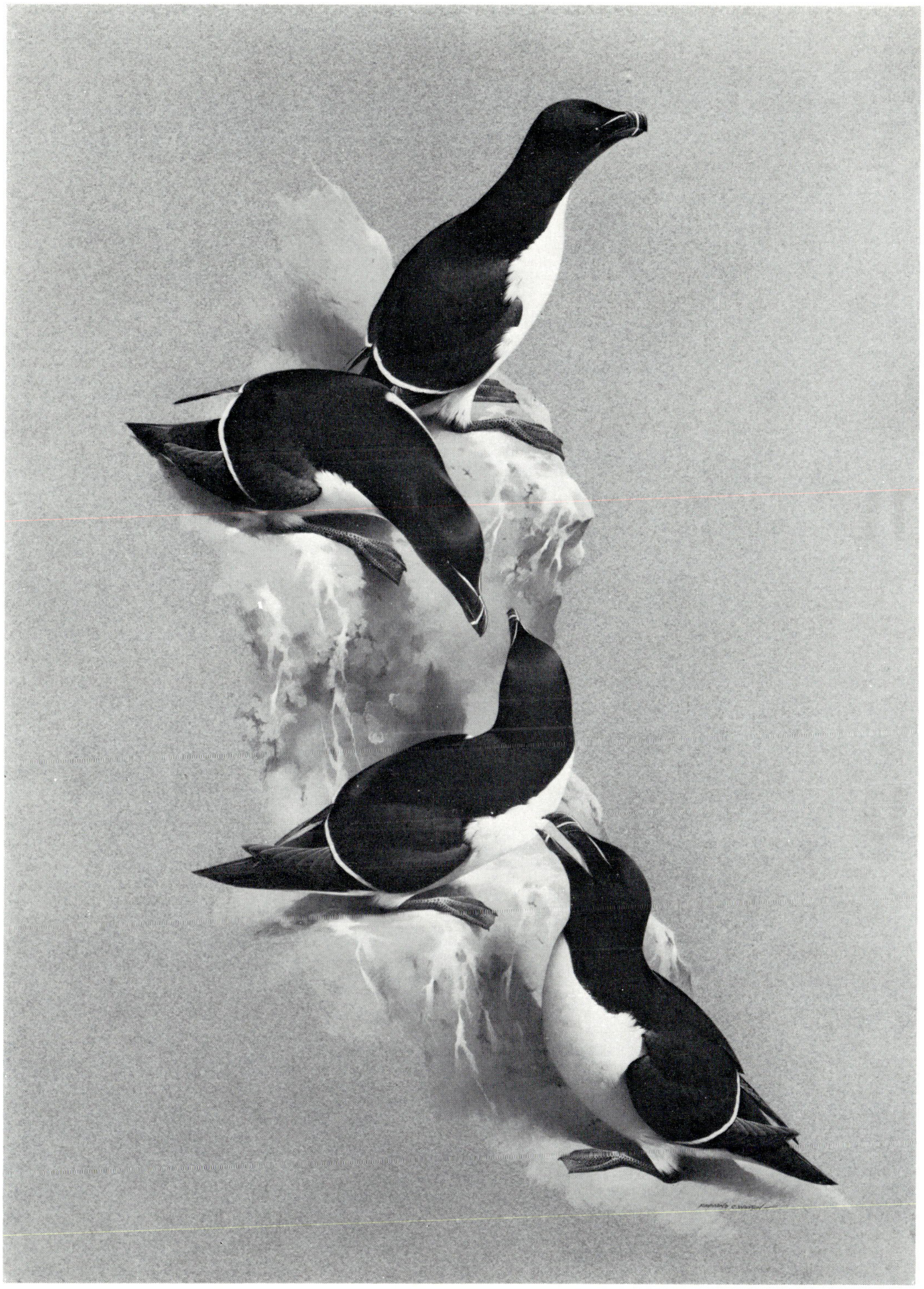

RAYMOND C. WATSON
Razorbills
Courtesy, The Moorland Gallery Ltd, London

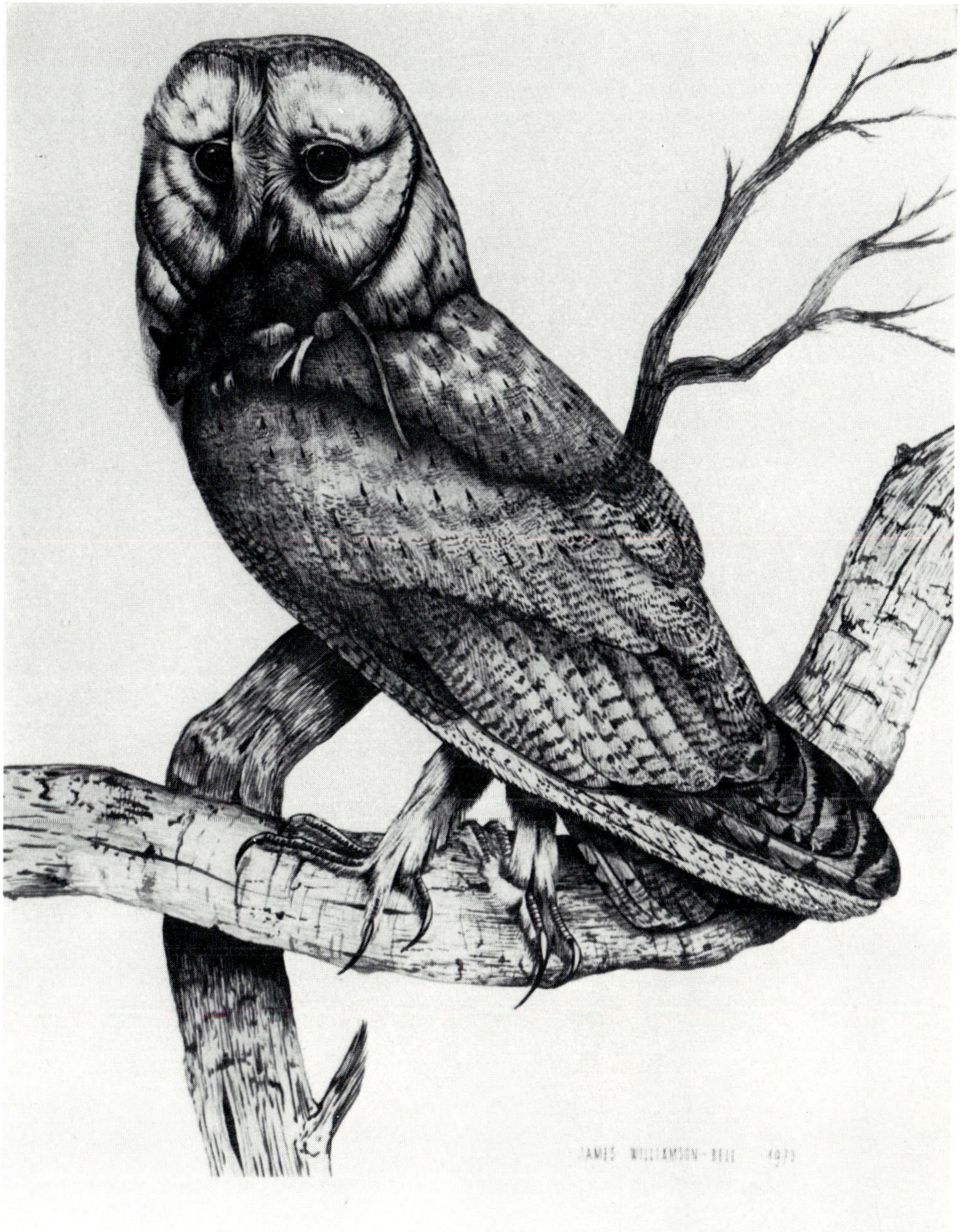

JAMES WILLIAMSON-BELL
Barn Owl

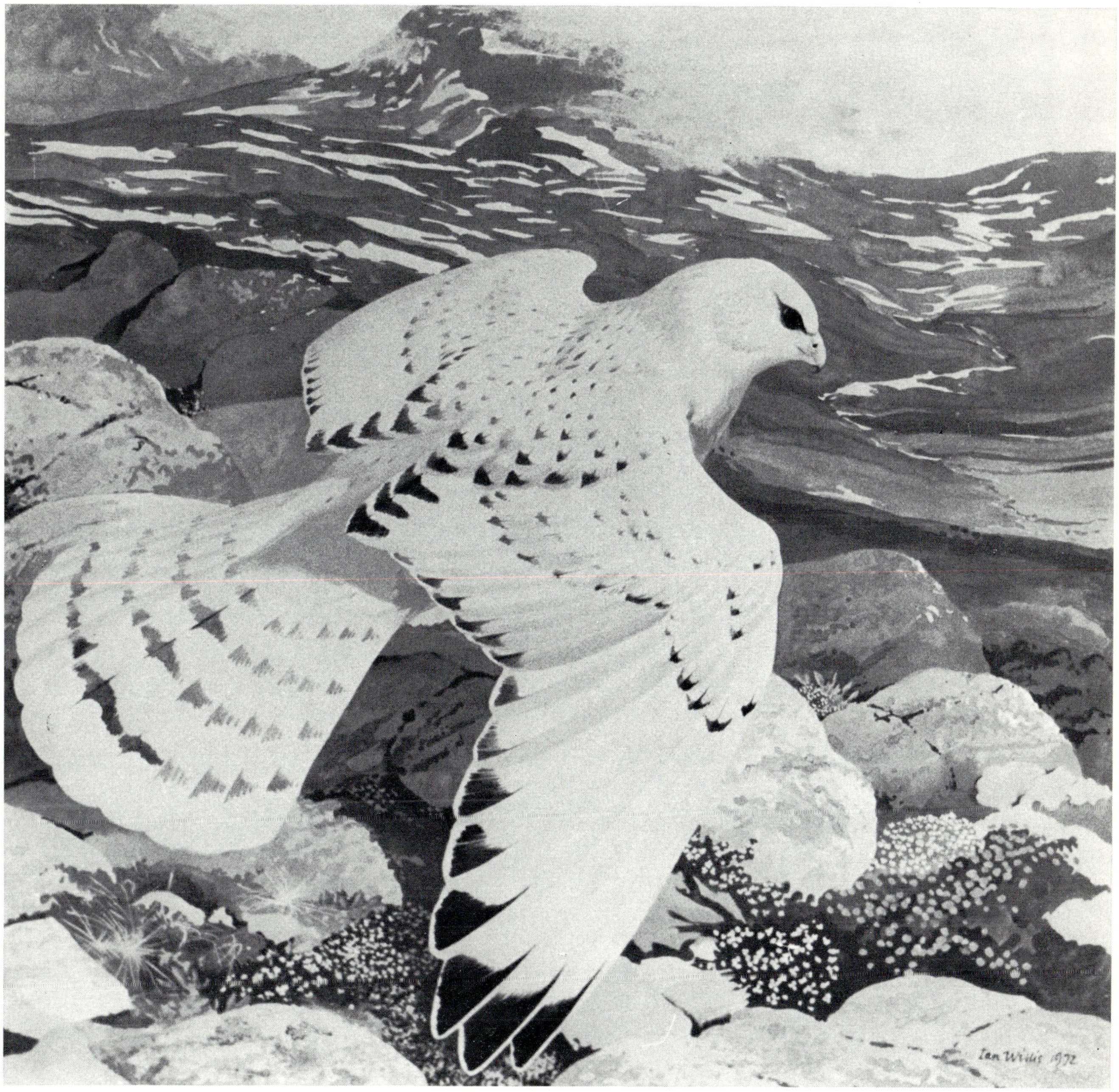

IAN ROBERT WILLIS
Gyr Falcon (white phase)